New American Short Stories

John Updike · Flannery O'Connor
John Cheever · Saul Bellow
Bernard Malamud · Joyce Carol Oates

Edited by Peter Bruck

Ernst Klett Stuttgart

Herausgegeben von Dr. Peter Bruck, Bochum,
unter Mitwirkung der Verlagsredaktion Neue Sprachen.
Mitarbeit an diesem Buch: Dr. Hartmut K. Selke, Verlagsredakteur.

Acknowledgments

John Updike, "A & P", copyright © by John Updike. Reprinted from *Pigeon Feathers and Other Stories*, by John Updike, by permission of Alfred A. Knopf, Inc., New York. Originally appeared in *The New Yorker*.

Flannery O'Connor, "Everything That Rises Must Converge", from *Everything That Rises Must Converge* (1965), is reprinted by permission of Farrar, Straus & Giroux, Inc., New York. Originally appeared in *New World Writing* in 1961.

John Cheever, "The Enormous Radio", copyright 1947 by John Cheever. Reprinted from *The Stories of John Cheever*, by John Cheever, by permission of Alfred A. Knopf, Inc., New York.

Saul Bellow, "A Father-to-Be", from *Mosby's Memoirs* (Viking Press, New York 1968), is reprinted by permission of Mohrbooks Literary Agency, Zurich. Originally appeared in *The New Yorker* in 1955.

Bernard Malamud, "The Mourners", from *The Magic Barrel* (1958), is reprinted by permission of Farrar, Straus & Giroux, Inc., New York.

Joyce Carol Oates, "Out of Place", from *The Seduction and Other Stories* (Black Sparrow Press, Los Angeles 1976), is reprinted by permission of Mohrbooks Literary Agency, Zurich. Originally appeared in *The Virginia Quarterly Review* in 1968.

The following stories of this collection are also available on cassette: John Updike, "A & P"; Saul Bellow, "A Father-to-Be"; Bernard Malamud, "The Mourners" (Klettnummer 57747).

ISBN 3-12-577400-4

1. Auflage   1 5 4 3 2 1 | 1987 86 85 84 83

Alle Drucke dieser Auflage können im Unterricht nebeneinander benutzt werden. Die letzte Zahl bezeichnet das Jahr dieses Druckes.
© dieser Ausgabe Ernst Klett, Stuttgart, 1983. Alle Rechte vorbehalten.
Umschlaggestaltung: Hans Lämmle, Stuttgart.
Druck: Gutmann & Co., Heilbronn. Printed in Germany.

Contents

Introduction 4

John Updike   *A & P* 5
Biography and Annotations 10

Flannery O'Connor   *Everything That Rises Must Converge* 13
Biography and Annotations 26

John Cheever   *The Enormous Radio* 29
Biography and Annotations 38

Saul Bellow   *A Father-to-Be* 41
Biography and Annotations 49

Bernard Malamud   *The Mourners* 52
Biography and Annotations 58

Joyce Carol Oates   *Out of Place* 60
Biography and Annotations 69

Introduction

The history of the American short story is usually considered to begin in 1819, when Washington Irving's *Sketch Book* was published. The new literary genre reached its first peak in the middle of the 19th century when Nathaniel Hawthorne, Edgar Allan Poe and Herman Melville produced a considerable body of short fiction. In the 20th century, the genre entered another period of fruition as Sherwood Anderson, Ernest Hemingway and William Faulkner became masters of the craft. While some of these writers are available in *Great American Short Stories* (Klett), this present collection, by contrast, consists of stories written between 1947 and 1968.

The six stories printed here have been selected with the following objectives in mind. They provide the reader with a representative, though necessarily limited, introduction to the contemporary American short story, its wide range of themes and some of its basic literary conventions. In addition, the stories offer insights into various aspects of contemporary American life-styles, manners and modes of experiencing social and political reality. The six stories can be divided into three sections according to the themes dealt with.
  I. Young People Confronting the World ("A & P", "Everything That Rises Must Converge"). In the first two stories the protagonists experience what they feel to be decisive moments in their lives.
  II. Aspects of Human Relations ("The Enormous Radio", "A Father-to-Be", "The Mourners"). The stories in this section depict various facets of interpersonal relationships in different social and ethnic surroundings.
  III. The War Experience ("Out of Place"). The final story deals with the fate of a Vietnam War veteran.

The American spelling of the stories has been retained and American spelling is used in the Annotations. The following abbreviations are used:
A.E.   American English   *dial.*   dialect
B.E.   British English   *fig.*   figurative
coll. colloquial   *sl.*   slang

Numbers in bold-face type in the margin refer to the corresponding pages in the text, those in light-face type to the lines of the respective page. Example **8** 32 = page 8, line 32.

John Updike
A & P

In walks these three girls in nothing but bathing suits. I'm in the third checkout slot, with my back to the door, so I don't see them until they're over by the bread. The one that caught my eye first was the one in the plaid green two-piece. She was a chunky kid, with a good tan and a sweet broad soft-looking can with those two crescents of white just under it, where the sun never seems to hit, at the top of the backs of her legs. I stood there with my hand on a box of HiHo crackers trying to remember if I rang it up or not. I ring it up again and the customer starts giving me hell. She's one of these cash-register-watchers, a witch about fifty with rouge on her cheekbones and no eyebrows, and I know it made her day to trip me up. She'd been watching cash registers for fifty years and probably never seen a mistake before.

By the time I got her feathers smoothed and her goodies into a bag — she gives me a little snort in passing, if she'd been born at the right time they would have burned her over in Salem – by the time I get her on her way the girls had circled around the bread and were coming back, without a pushcart, back my way along the counters, in the aisle between the checkouts and the Special bins. They didn't even have shoes on. There was this chunky one, with the two-piece — it was bright green and the seams on the bra were still sharp and her belly was still pretty pale so I guessed she just got it (the suit) — there was this one, with one of those chubby berry-faces, the lips all bunched together under her nose, this one, and a tall one, with black hair that hadn't quite frizzed right, and one of these sunburns right across under the eyes, and a chin that was too long — you know, the kind of girl other girls think is very "striking" and "attractive" but never quite makes it, as they very well know, which is why they like her so much — and then the third one, that wasn't quite so tall. She was the queen. She kind of led them, the other two peeking around and making their shoulders round. She didn't look around, not this queen, she just walked straight on slowly, on these long white prima-donna legs. She came down a little hard on her heels, as if she didn't walk in her bare feet that much, putting down her heels and then letting the weight move along to her toes as if she was testing the floor with every step, putting a little deliberate extra action into it. You never know for sure how girls' minds work (do you really think it's a mind in there or just a little buzz like a bee in a glass jar?) but you got the idea she had talked the other two into coming in here with her, and now she was showing them how to do it, walk slow and hold yourself straight.

She had on a kind of dirty-pink — beige maybe, I don't know — bathing suit with a little nubble all over it and, what got me, the straps were down. They were off her shoulders looped loose around the cool tops of her arms, and I guess as a result the suit had slipped a little on her, so all around the top of the cloth there was this shining rim. If it hadn't been there you wouldn't have known there could have been anything whiter than those shoulders. With the straps pushed off, there was nothing between the top of the suit and the top of her head except just *her*, this clean bare plane of the top of her chest down from the shoulder bones like a dented sheet of metal tilted in the light. I mean, it was more than pretty.

She had sort of oaky hair that the sun and salt had bleached, done up in a bun that was unraveling, and a kind of prim face. Walking into the A & P with your straps down, I suppose it's the only kind of face you *can* have. She held her head so high her neck, coming up out of those white shoulders, looked kind of stretched, but I didn't mind. The longer her neck was, the more of her there was.

She must have felt in the corner of her eye me and over my shoulder Stokesie in the second slot watching, but she didn't tip. Not this queen. She kept her eyes moving across the racks, and stopped, and turned so slow it made my stomach rub the inside of my apron, and buzzed to the other two, who kind of huddled against her for relief, and then they all three of them went up the cat-and-dog-food-breakfast-cereal-macaroni-rice-raisins-seasonings-spreads-spaghetti-soft-drinks-crackers-and-cookies aisle. From the third slot I look straight up this aisle to the meat counter, and I watched them all the way. The fat one with the tan sort of fumbled with the cookies, but on second thought she put the package back. The sheep pushing their carts down the aisle — the girls were walking against the usual traffic (not that we have one-way signs or anything) — were pretty hilarious. You could see them, when Queenie's white shoulders dawned on them, kind of jerk, or hop, or hiccup, but their eyes snapped back to their own baskets and on they pushed. I bet you could set off dynamite in an A & P and the people would by and large keep reaching and checking oatmeal off their lists and muttering "Let me see, there was a third thing, began with A, asparagus, no, ah, yes, applesauce!"or whatever it is they do mutter. But here was no doubt, this jiggled them. A few houseslaves in pin curlers even looked around after pushing their carts past to make sure what they had seen was correct.

You know, it's one thing to have a girl in a bathing suit down on the beach, where what with the glare nobody can look at each other much anyway, and another thing in the cool of the A & P, under the fluorescent lights, against all those stacked packages, with her feet paddling along naked over our checkerboard green-and-cream rubber-tile floor.

"Oh Daddy," Stokesie said beside me. "I feel so faint."

"Darling," I said. "Hold me tight." Stokesie's married, with two babies chalked up on his fuselage already, but as far as I can tell that's the only difference. He's twenty-two, and I was nineteen this April.

"Is it done?" he asks, the responsible married man finding his voice. I forgot to say he thinks he's going to be manager some sunny day, maybe in 1990 when it's called the Great Alexandrov and Petrooshki Tea Company or something.

What he meant was, our town is five miles from a beach, with a big summer colony out on the Point, but we're right in the middle of town, and the women generally put on a shirt or shorts or something before they get out of the car into the street. And anyway these are usually women with six children and varicose veins mapping their legs and nobody, including them, could care less. As I say, we're right in the middle of town, and if you stand at our front doors you can see two banks and the Congregational church and the newspaper store and three real-estate offices and about twenty-seven old freeloaders tearing up Central Street because the sewer broke again. It's not as if we're on the Cape; we're north of Boston and there's people in this town haven't seen the ocean for twenty years.

The girls had reached the meat counter and were asking McMahon something. He pointed, they pointed, and they shuffled out of sight behind a pyramid of Diet Delight peaches. All that was left for us to see was old McMahon patting his mouth and looking after them sizing up their joints. Poor kids, I began to feel sorry for them, they couldn't help it.

Now here comes the sad part of the story, at least my family says it's sad, but I don't think it's so sad myself. The store's pretty empty, it being Thursday afternoon, so there was nothing much to do except lean on the register and wait for the girls to show up again. The whole store was like a pinball machine and I didn't know which tunnel they'd come out of. After a while they come around out of the far aisle, around the light bulbs, records at discount of the Caribbean Six or Tony Martin Sings or some such gunk you wonder they waste the wax on, sixpacks of candy bars, and plastic toys done up in cellophane that fall apart when a kid looks at them anyway. Around they come, Queenie still leading the way, and holding a little gray jar in her hand. Slots Three through Seven are unmanned and I could see her wondering between Stokes and me, but Stokesie with his usual luck draws an old party in baggy gray pants who stumbles up with four giant cans of pineapple juice (what do these bums *do* with all that pineapple juice? I've often asked myself) so the girls come to me. Queenie puts down the jar and I take it into my fingers icy cold. Kingfish Fancy Herring Snacks in Pure Sour Cream: 49 ¢. Now her hands are empty, not a ring or a bracelet, bare as God made them, and I wonder where the money's coming from. Still with that prim look she lifts a folded dollar bill out of the hollow at the center of her nubbled pink top. The jar went heavy in my hand. Really, I thought that was so cute.

Then everybody's luck begins to run out. Lengel comes in from haggling with a truck full of cabbages on the lot and is about to scuttle into that door marked MANAGER behind which he hides all day when the girls touch his eye. Lengel's pretty dreary, teaches Sunday school and the rest, but he doesn't miss that much. He comes over and says, "Girls, this isn't the beach."

Queenie blushes, though maybe it's just a brush of sunburn I was noticing for the first time, now that she was so close. "My mother asked me to pick up a jar of herring snacks." Her voice kind of startled me, the way voices do when you see the people first, coming out so flat and dumb yet kind of tony, too, the way it ticked over "pick up" and "snacks." All of a sudden I slid right down her voice into her living room. Her father and the other men were standing around in ice-cream coats and bow ties and the women were in sandals picking up herring snacks on toothpicks off a big glass plate and they were all holding drinks the color of water with olives and sprigs of mint in them. When my parents have somebody over they get lemonade and if it's a real racy affair Schlitz in tall glasses with "They'll Do It Every Time" cartoons stenciled on.

"That's all right," Lengel said. "But this isn't the beach." His repeating this struck me as funny, as if it had just occurred to him, and he had been thinking all these years the A & P was a great big sand dune and he was the head lifeguard. He didn't like my smiling — as I say he doesn't miss much – but he concentrates on giving the girls that sad Sunday-school-superintendent stare.

Queenie's blush is no sunburn now, and the plump one in plaid, that I liked better from the back — a really sweet can — pipes up, "We weren't doing any shopping. We just came in for the one thing."

"That makes no difference," Lengel tells her, and I could see from the way his eyes went that he hadn't noticed she was wearing a two-piece before. "We want you decently dressed when you come in here."

"We *are* decent," Queenie says suddenly, her lower lip pushing, getting sore now that she remembers her place, a place from which the crowd that runs the A & P must look pretty crummy. Fancy Herring Snacks flashed in her very blue eyes.

"Girls, I don't want to argue with you. After this come in here with your shoulders covered. It's our policy." He turns his back. That's policy for you. Policy is what the kingpins want. What the others want is juvenile delinquency.

All this while, the customers had been showing up with their carts but, you know, sheep, seeing a scene, they had all bunched up on Stokesie, who shook open a paper bag as gently as peeling a peach, not wanting to miss a word. I could feel in the silence everybody getting nervous, most of all Lengel, who asks me, "Sammy, have you rung up their purchase?"

I thought and said "No" but it wasn't about that I was thinking. I go through the punches, 4, 9, GROC, TOT — it's more complicated than you think, and after you do it often enough, it begins to make a little song, that you hear words to, in my case "Hello *(bing)* there, you *(gung)* hap-py pee-pul *(splat)*!" — the *splat* being the drawer flying out. I uncrease the bill, tenderly as you may imagine, it just having come from between the two smoothest scoops of vanilla I had ever known were there, and pass a half and a penny into her narrow pink palm, and nestle the herrings in a bag and twist its neck and hand it over, all the time thinking.

The girls, and who'd blame them, are in a hurry to get out, so I say "I quit" to Lengel quick enough for them to hear, hoping they'll stop and watch me, their unsuspected hero. They keep right on going, into the electric eye; the door flies open and they flicker across the lot to their car, Queenie and Plaid and Big Tall Goony-Goony (not that as raw material she was so bad), leaving me with Lengel and a kink in his eyebrow.

"Did you say something, Sammy?"
"I said I quit."
"I thought you did."
"You didn't have to embarrass them."
"It was they who were embarrassing us."

I started to say something that came out "Fiddle-de-doo." It's a saying of my grandmother's, and I know she would have been pleased.

"I don't think you know what you're saying," Lengel said.

"I know you don't," I said. "But I do." I pull the bow at the back of my apron and start shrugging it off my shoulders. A couple customers that had been heading for my slot begin to knock against each other, like scared pigs in a chute.

Lengel sighs and begins to look very patient and old and gray. He's been a friend of my parents for years. "Sammy, you don't want to do this to your Mom and Dad," he tells me. It's true, I don't. But it seems to me that once you begin a gesture it's fatal not to go through with it. I fold the apron, "Sammy" stitched in red on the pocket, and put it on the counter, and drop the bow tie on top of it. The bow tie is theirs, if you've ever wondered.

"You'll feel this for the rest of your life," Lengel says, and I know that's true, too, but remembering how he made that pretty girl blush makes me so scrunchy inside I punch the No Sale tab and the machine whirs "pee-pul" and the drawer splats out. One advantage to this scene taking place in summer, I can follow this up with a clean exit, there's no fumbling around getting your coat and galoshes, I just saunter into the electric eye in my white shirt that my mother ironed the night before, and the door heaves itself open, and outside the sunshine is skating around on the asphalt.

I look around for my girls, but they're gone, of course. There wasn't anybody but some young married screaming with her children about some candy they didn't get by the door of a powder-blue Falcon station wagon. Looking back in the big windows, over the bags of peat moss and aluminum lawn furniture stacked on the pavement, I could see Lengel in my place in the slot, checking the sheep through. His face was dark gray and his back stiff, as if he'd just had an injection of iron, and my stomach kind of fell as I felt how hard the world was going to be to me hereafter.

Biographical Notes

John Updike (born 1932) grew up in Pennsylvania and later attended Harvard College. From 1955 to 1957 he was a staff member of The New Yorker, *to which he has contributed stories, essays and poems. In addition to his many novels, Updike has published five collections of short stories to date, most of which describe the manners and life-style of the American middle class. As he once put it, "My subject is the American Protestant small-town middle class. It is in middles that extremes clash, where ambiguity restlessly rules."*

"A & P" first appeared in The New Yorker *in 1961 and was later included in the collection* Pigeon Feathers and Other Stories *(1962).*

Annotations

5 **A & P** *short for:* Atlantic and Pacific Tea Company, a chain of supermarkets – 2 **checkout slot** desk in a supermarket where one pays for the goods – 3 **plaid** [æ] square-patterned – 4 **chunky** short and fat – **tan** brown color of sunburnt skin – 5 **can** *sl.* behind – **crescent** ['kresnt] shape of the moon when it forms less than half a circle – 7 **cracker** a thin, crisp biscuit – **to ring up** to record the price of goods on a cash register – 9 **witch** an ugly old woman – 10 **it made her day** it gave her great pleasure – **to trip s.o. up** to catch s.o. making a mistake – 13 **to smooth s.o.'s feathers** to calm s.o. – **goodies** *coll.* any goods – 14 **snort** sudden breath forced through the nostrils to express anger – 15 **Salem** [eɪ] seaport in Massachusetts where "witches" were tried and burnt in 1692 – 17 **aisle** [aɪl] narrow passage – 18 **Special bin** *here:* container for goods on special offer – 19 **seam** line formed by sewing together two pieces of cloth – 21 **chubby** slightly fat – 23 **to frizz** to form into small curls – 28 **to peek** to take a short, quick look

6 7 **nubble** small lump or knob – **what got me** *coll.* what shocked, annoyed or (as in this case) pleased me – **strap** band used as fastening – 8 **looped** *here:* hanging so that the strap is folded across itself – 10 **rim** edge – 13 **plane** even surface – 14 **dented** having holes or hollows made by blows or pressure – 16 **oaky** of the colour of oak-wood – 17 **bun** hair twisted into a tight round shape above the neck – **unraveling** *here:* about to come undone – **prim** showing dislike of anything rough or rude – 23 **to tip** *here:* to react, to show that one notices s.th. – 31 **sheep** *here:* the customers who go round the usual way – 33 **hilarious** [hɪ'leərɪəs] funny, causing laughter – 34 **to dawn on s.b.** *here:* to begin to notice – **jerk** sharp abrupt movement – 35 **hiccup** sudden stopping of the breath causing one to make a sharp sound – 37 **by and large** on the whole – **oatmeal** food made from oats (Hafergrütze) – 40 **to jiggle** *coll.* to surprise, to amaze

7 4 **what with** because of – 5 **fluorescent light** [ˌfluːə'resnt] neon light – 7 **checkerboard** patterned in squares – 10 **to chalk up** to record – **fuselage** ['fjuːzəlɑːʒ] body of an aircraft (reference to pilots who chalked up the number of planes they had shot down on the side of their aircraft) – 20 **varicose vein** [veɪn] blood-vessel that has become permanently enlarged – 22 **Congregational Church** a Protestant denomination in which each member church is self-governing – 23 **real estate** (buying and selling of) houses and land – 24 **freeloader** *sl.* person who expects free food, services, etc. – **sewer** underground pipe carrying waste water – 25 **the Cape** Cape Cod on the coast of Massachusetts – 30 **to size up** *coll.* to look over in order to form an opinion of – **joint** shoulder or leg of meat sold by a butcher – 36 **pinball machine** machine with a sloping board down which a rolling ball is guided by various means – 38 **gunk** *sl.* horrible sticky or slimy matter – 39 **wax** *here:* material originally used for making records

8 5 **party** *here:* customer – **baggy** hanging loosely – 6 **bum** *coll.* worthless person – 8 **fancy** not ordinary, made to taste good – 14 **to haggle** to argue over the price – 15 **lot** parking area – **to scuttle** to move hastily – 17 **dreary** dull – 21 **to startle** to shock slightly, to surprise – 22 **tony** high-toned, stylish – 23 **to slide** to slip along, to move smoothly over – 25 **bow tie** [əʊ] tie in the form of a bow, not hanging down – 27 **sprig** piece, small twig with leaves – 29 **racy** *here:* special, stylish – **Schlitz** a brand of beer

9 5 **crummy** *coll.* of poor quality, shabby – 9 **kingpin** *coll.* most important person, boss – **juvenile delinquency** crimes committed by young people – 12 **to bunch up** to group together – 17 **punch** *here:* key of a cash register – **GROC** groceries – **TOT** sum total – 20 **to uncrease** [s] to unfold, to flatten out – 22 **scoop** a large round spoon for serving out ice cream; *also:* the ball of ice cream served in this way – 29 **goon** a stupid person – **Goony** a grotesque comic-strip character – 30 **kink** twist or bend – 36 **fiddle-de-doo** *interj.* nonsense

10 2 **chute** [ʃuːt] a channel which transports s.th. downwards – 11 **scrunchy** *here:* hurt – **tab** *here:* key of a cash register – **to whir** (*B.E.* whirr) to make a sound as of wheels turning fast – 14 **to saunter** to walk unhurriedly – 19 **station wagon** car made to carry both people and goods – 20 **peat moss** special carth used for planting flowers or for seed beds

Flannery O'Connor

Everything That Rises Must Converge

Her doctor had told Julian's mother that she must lose twenty pounds on account of her blood pressure, so on Wednesday nights Julian had to take her downtown on the bus for a reducing class at the Y. The reducing class was designed for working girls over fifty, who weighed from 165 to 200 pounds. His mother was one of the slimmer ones, but she said ladies did not tell their age or weight. She would not ride the buses by herself at night since they had been integrated, and because the reducing class was one of her few pleasures, necessary for her health, and *free*, she said Julian could at least put himself out to take her, considering all she did for him. Julian did not like to consider all she did for him, but every Wednesday night he braced himself and took her.

She was almost ready to go, standing before the hall mirror, putting on her hat, while he, his hands behind him, appeared pinned to the door frame, waiting like Saint Sebastian for the arrows to begin piercing him. The hat was new and had cost her seven dollars and a half. She kept saying, "Maybe I shouldn't have paid that for it. No, I shouldn't have. I'll take it off and return it tomorrow. I shouldn't have bought it."

Julian raised his eyes to heaven. "Yes, you should have bought it," he said. "Put it on and let's go." It was a hideous hat. A purple velvet flap came down on one side of it and stood up on the other; the rest of it was green and looked like a cushion with the stuffing out. He decided it was less comical than jaunty and pathetic. Everything that gave her pleasure was small and depressed him.

She lifted the hat one more time and set it down slowly on top of her head. Two wings of gray hair protruded on either side of her florid face, but her eyes, sky-blue, were as innocent and untouched by experience as they must have been when she was ten. Were it not that she was a widow who had struggled fiercely to feed and clothe and put him through school and who was supporting him still, "until he got on his feet," she might have been a little girl that he had to take to town.

"It's all right, it's all right," he said. "Let's go." He opened the door himself and started down the walk to get her going. The sky was a dying violet and the houses stood out darkly against it, bulbous liver-colored monstrosities of a uniform ugliness though no two were alike. Since this had been a fashionable neighborhood forty years ago, his mother persisted in thinking they did well to have an apartment in it. Each house had a narrow collar of dirt around it in which sat, usually, a grubby child. Julian walked with his hands in his pockets, his head down and thrust forward and his eyes glazed with the determination to make himself completely numb during the time he would be sacrificed to her pleasure.

The door closed and he turned to find the dumpy figure, surmounted by the atrocious hat, coming toward him. "Well," she said, "you only live once and paying a little more for it, I at least won't meet myself coming and going."

"Some day I'll start making money," Julian said gloomily — he knew he never would — "and you can have one of those jokes whenever you take the fit." But first they would move. He visualized a place where the nearest neighbors would be three miles away on either side.

"I think you're doing fine," she said, drawing on her gloves. "You've only been out of school a year. Rome wasn't built in a day."

She was one of the few members of the Y reducing class who arrived in hat and gloves and who had a son who had been to college. "It takes time," she said, "and the world is in such a mess. This hat looked better on me than any of the others, though when she brought it out I said, 'Take that thing back. I wouldn't have it on my head,' and she said, 'Now wait till you see it on,' and when she put it on me, I said, 'We-ull,' and she said. 'If you ask me, that hat does something for you and you do something for the hat, and besides,' she said, 'with that hat, you won't meet yourself coming and going.'"

Julian thought he could have stood his lot better if she had been selfish, if she had been an old hag who drank and screamed at him. He walked along, saturated in depression, as if in the midst of his martyrdom he had lost his faith. Catching sight of his long, hopeless, irritated face, she stopped suddenly with a grief-stricken look, and pulled back on his arm. "Wait on me," she said. "I'm going back to the house and take this thing off and tomorrow I'm going to return it. I was out of my head. I can pay the gas bill with that seven-fifty."

He caught her arm in a vicious grip. "You are not going to take it back," he said. "I like it."

"Well," she said, "I don't think I ought..."

"Shut up and enjoy it," he muttered, more depressed than ever.

"With the world in the mess it's in," she said, "it's a wonder we can enjoy anything. I tell you, the bottom rail is on the top."

Julian sighed.

"Of course," she said, "if you know who you are, you can go anywhere." She said this every time he took her to the reducing class. "Most of them in it are not our kind of people," she said, "but I can be gracious to anybody. I know who I am."

"They don't give a damn for your graciousness," Julian said savagely. "Knowing who you are is good for one generation only. You haven't the foggiest idea where you stand now or who you are."

She stopped and allowed her eyes to flash at him. "I most certainly do know who I am," she said, "and if you don't know who you are, I'm ashamed of you."

"Oh hell," Julian said.

"Your great-grandfather was a former governor of this state," she said. "Your grandfather was a prosperous landowner. Your grandmother was a Godhigh."

"Will you look around you," he said tensely, "and see where you are now?" and he swept his arm jerkily out to indicate the neighborhood, which the growing darkness at least made less dingy.

"You remain what you are," she said. "Your great-grandfather had a plantation and two hundred slaves."

"There are no more slaves," he said irritably.

"They were better off when they were," she said. He groaned to see that she was off on that topic. She rolled onto it every few days like a train on an open track. He knew every stop, every junction, every swamp along the way, and knew the exact point at which her conclusion would roll majestically into the station: "It's ridiculous. It's simply not realistic. They should rise, yes, but on their own side of the fence."

"Let's skip it," Julian said.

"The ones I feel sorry for," she said, "are the ones that are half white. They're tragic."

"Will you skip it?"

"Suppose we were half white. We would certainly have mixed feelings."

"I have mixed feelings now," he groaned.

"Well let's talk about something pleasant," she said. "I remember going to Grandpa's when I was a little girl. Then the house had double stairways that went up to what was really the second floor — all the cooking was done on the first. I used to like to stay down in the kitchen on account of the way the walls smelled. I would sit with my nose pressed against the plaster and take deep breaths. Actually the place belonged to the Godhighs but your grandfather Chestny paid the mortgage and saved it for them. They were in reduced circumstances," she said, "but reduced or not, they never forgot who they were."

"Doubtless that decayed mansion reminded them," Julian muttered. He never spoke of it without contempt or thought of it without longing. He had seen it once when he was a child before it had been sold. The double stairways had rotted and been torn down. Negroes were living in it. But it remained in his mind as his mother had known it. It appeared in his dreams regularly. He would stand on the wide porch, listening to the rustle of oak leaves, then wander through the high-ceilinged hall into the parlor that opened onto it and gaze at the worn rugs and faded draperies. It occurred to him that it was he, not she, who could have appreciated it. He preferred its threadbare elegance to anything he could name and it was because of it that all the neighborhoods they had lived in had been a torment to him — whereas she had hardly known the difference. She called her insensitivity "being adjustable."

"And I remember the old darky who was my nurse, Caroline. There was no better person in the world. I've always had a great respect for my colored friends," she said. "I'd do anything in the world for them and they'd..."

"Will you for God's sake get off that subject?" Julian said. When he got on a bus by himself, he made it a point to sit down beside a Negro, in reparation as it were for his mother's sins.

"You're mighty touchy tonight," she said. "Do you feel all right?"

"Yes I feel all right," he said. " Now lay off."

She pursed her lips. "Well, you certainly are in a vile humor," she observed. "I just won't speak to you at all."

They had reached the bus stop. There was no bus in sight and Julian, his hands still jammed in his pockets and his head thrust forward, scowled down the empty street. The frustration of having to wait on the bus as well as ride on it began to creep up his neck like a hot hand. The presence of his mother was borne in upon him as she gave a pained sigh. He looked at her bleakly. She was holding herself very erect under the preposterous hat, wearing it like a banner of her imaginary dignity. There was in him an evil urge to break her spirit. He suddenly unloosened his tie and pulled it off and put it in his pocket.

She stiffened. "Why must you look like *that* when you take me to town?" she said. "Why must you deliberately embarrass me?"

"If you'll never learn where you are," he said, "you can at least learn where I am."

"You look like a — thug," she said.

"Then I must be one," he murmured.

"I'll just go home," she said. "I will not bother you. If you can't do a little thing like that for me ..."

Rolling his eyes upward, he put his tie back on. "Restored to my class," he muttered. He thrust his face toward her and hissed, "True culture is in the mind, the *mind*," he said, and tapped his head, "the mind."

"It's in the heart," she said, "and in how you do things and how you do things is because of who you *are*."

"Nobody in the damn bus cares who you are."

"I care who I am," she said icily.

The lighted bus appeared on top of the next hill and as it approached, they moved out into the street to meet it. He put his hand under her elbow and hoisted her up on the creaking step. She entered with a little smile, as if she were going into a drawing room where everyone had been waiting for her. While he put in the tokens, she sat down on one of the broad front seats for three which faced the aisle. A thin woman with protruding teeth and long yellow hair was sitting on the end of it. His mother moved up beside her and left room for Julian beside herself. He sat down and looked at the floor across the aisle where a pair of thin feet in red and white canvas sandals were planted.

His mother immediately began a general conversation meant to attract anyone who felt like talking. "Can it get any hotter?" she said and removed from her purse a folding fan, black with a Japanese scene on it, which she began to flutter before her.

"I reckon it might could," the woman with the protruding teeth said, "but I know for a fact my apartment couldn't get no hotter."

"It must get the afternoon sun," his mother said. She sat forward and looked up and down the bus. It was half filled. Everybody was white. "I see we have the bus to ourselves," she said. Julian cringed.

"For a change," said the woman across the aisle, the owner of the red and white canvas sandals. "I come on one the other day and they were thick as fleas — up front and all through."

"The world is in a mess everywhere," his mother said. "I don't know how we've let it get in this fix."

"What gets my goat is all those boys from good families stealing automobile tires," the woman with the protruding teeth said. "I told my boy, I said you may not be rich but you been raised right and if I ever catch you in any such mess, they can send you on to the reformatory. Be exactly where you belong."

"Training tells," his mother said. "Is your boy in high school?"

"Ninth grade," the woman said.

"My son just finished college last year. He wants to write but he's selling typewriters until he gets started," his mother said.

The woman leaned forward and peered at Julian. He threw her such a malevolent look she subsided against the seat. On the floor across the aisle there was an abandoned newspaper. He got up and got it and opened it out in front of him. His mother discreetly continued the conversation in a lower tone but the woman across the aisle said in a loud voice. "Well that's nice. Selling typewriters is close to writing. He can go right from one to the other."

"I tell him," his mother said, "that Rome wasn't built in a day."

Behind the newspaper Julian was withdrawing into the inner compartment of his mind where he spent most of his time. This was a kind of mental bubble in which he established himself when he could not bear to be a part of what was going on around him. From it he could see out and judge but in it he was safe from any kind of penetration from without. It was the only place where he felt free of the general idiocy of his fellows. His mother had never entered it but from it he could see her with absolute clarity.

The old lady was clever enough and he thought that if she had started from any of the right premises, more might have been expected of her. She lived according to the laws of her own fantasy world, outside of which he had never seen her set foot. The law of it was to sacrifice herself for him after she had first created the necessity to do so by making a mess of things. If he had permitted her sacrifices, it was only because her lack of foresight had made them necessary. All of her life had been a struggle to act like a Chestny without the Chestny goods, and to give him everything she thought a Chestny ought to have; but since, said she, it was fun to struggle, why complain? And when you had won, as she had won, what fun to look back on the hard times! He could not forgive her that she had enjoyed the struggle and that she thought *she* had won.

What she meant when she said she had won was that she had brought him up successfully and had sent him to college and that he had turned out so well — good looking (her teeth had gone unfilled so that his could be straightened), intelligent (he realized he was too intelligent to be a success), and with a future ahead of him (there was of course no future ahead of him). She excused his gloominess on the grounds that he was still growing up and his radical ideas on his lack of practical experience. She said he didn't yet know a thing about "life," that he hadn't even entered the real world — when already he was as disenchanted with it as a man of fifty.

The further irony of all this was that in spite of her, he had turned out so well. In spite of going to only a third-rate college, he had, on his own initiative, come out with a first-rate education; in spite of growing up dominated by a small mind, he had ended up with a large one; in spite of all her foolish views, he was free of prejudice and unafraid to face facts. Most miraculous of all, instead of being blinded by love for her as she was for him, he had cut himself emotionally free of her and could see her with complete objectivity. He was not dominated by his mother.

The bus stopped with a sudden jerk and shook him from his meditation. A woman from the back lurched forward with little steps and barely escaped falling in his newspaper as she righted herself. She got off and a large Negro got on. Julian kept his paper lowered to watch. It gave him a certain satisfaction to see injustice in daily operation. It confirmed his view that with a few exceptions there was no one worth knowing within a radius of three hundred miles. The Negro was well dressed and carried a briefcase. He looked around and then sat down on the other end of the seat where the woman with the red and white canvas sandals was sitting. He immediately unfolded a newspaper and obscured himself behind it. Julian's mother's elbow at once prodded insistently into his ribs. "Now you see why I won't ride on these buses by myself," she whispered.

The woman with the red and white canvas sandals had risen at the same time the Negro sat down and had gone further back in the bus and taken the seat of the woman who had got off. His mother leaned forward and cast her an approving look.

Julian rose, crossed the aisle, and sat down in the place of the woman with the canvas sandals. From this position, he looked serenely across at his mother. Her face had turned an angry red. He stared at her, making his eyes the eyes of a stranger. He felt his tension suddenly lift as if he had openly declared war on her.

He would have liked to get in conversation with the Negro and to talk with him about art or politics or any subject that would be above the comprehension of those around them, but the man remained entrenched behind his paper. He was either ignoring the change of seating or had never noticed it. There was no way for Julian to convey his sympathy.

His mother kept her eyes fixed reproachfully on his face. The woman with the protruding teeth was looking at him avidly as if he were a type of monster new to her.

"Do you have a light?" he asked the Negro.

Without looking away from his paper, the man reached in his pocket and handed him a packet of matches.

"Thanks," Julian said. For a moment he held the matches foolishly. A NO SMOKING sign looked down upon him from over the door. This alone would not have deterred him; he had no cigarettes. He had quit smoking some months before because he could not afford it. "Sorry," he muttered and handed back the matches. The Negro lowered the paper and gave him an annoyed look. He took the matches and raised the paper again.

His mother continued to gaze at him but she did not take advantage of his momentary discomfort. Her eyes retained their battered look. Her face seemed to be unnaturally red, as if her blood pressure had risen. Julian allowed no glimmer of sympathy to show on his face. Having got the advantage, he wanted desperately to keep it and carry it through. He would have liked to teach her a lesson that would last her a while, but there seemed no way to continue the point. The Negro refused to come out from behind his paper.

Julian folded his arms and looked stolidly before him, facing her but as if he did not see her, as if he had ceased to recognize her existence. He visualized a scene in which, the bus having reached their stop, he would remain in his seat and when she said, "Aren't you going to get off?" he would look at her as at a stranger who had rashly addressed him. The corner they got off on was usually deserted, but it was well lighted and it would not hurt her to walk by herself the four blocks to the Y. He decided to wait until the time came and then decide whether or not he would let her get off by herself. He would have to be at the Y at ten to bring her back, but he could leave her wondering if he was going to show up. There was no reason for her to think she could always depend on him.

He retired again into the high-ceilinged room sparsely settled with large pieces of antique furniture. His soul expanded momentarily but then he became aware of his mother across from him and the vision shriveled. He studied her coldly. Her feet in little pumps dangled like a child's and did not quite reach the floor. She was training on him an exaggerated look of reproach. He felt completely detached from her. At that moment he could with pleasure have slapped her as he would have slapped a particularly obnoxious child in his charge.

He began to imagine various unlikely ways by which he could teach her a lesson. He might make friends with some distinguished Negro professor or lawyer and bring him home to spend the evening. He would be entirely justified but her blood pressure would rise to 300. He could not push her to the extent of making her have a stroke, and moreover, he had never been successful at making any Negro friends. He had tried to strike up an acquaintance on the bus with some of the better types. One morning he had sat down next to a distinguished-looking dark brown man who had answered his questions with a sonorous solemnity but who had turned out to be an undertaker. Another day he had sat down beside a cigar-smoking Negro with a diamond ring on his finger, but after a few stilted pleasantries, the Negro had rung the buzzer and risen, slipping two lottery tickets into Julian's hand as he climbed over him to leave.

He imagined his mother lying desperately ill and his being able to secure only a Negro doctor for her. He toyed with that idea for a few minutes and then dropped it for a momentary vision of himself participating as a sympathizer in a sit-in demonstration. This was possible but he did not linger with it. Instead, he approached the ultimate horror. He brought home a beautiful suspiciously Negroid woman. Prepare yourself, he said. There is nothing you can do about it. This is the woman I've chosen. She's intelligent, dignified, even good, and she's suffered and she hasn't thought it *fun*. Now persecute us, go ahead and persecute us. Drive her out of here, but remember, you're driving me too. His eyes were narrowed and through the indignation he had generated, he saw his mother across the aisle, purple-faced, shrunken to the dwarf-like proportions of her moral nature, sitting like a mummy beneath the ridiculous banner of her hat.

He was tilted out of his fantasy again as the bus stopped. The door opened with a sucking hiss and out of the dark a large, gaily dressed, sullen-looking colored woman got on with a little boy. The child, who might have been four, had on a short plaid suit and a Tyrolean hat with a blue feather in it. Julian hoped that he would sit down beside him and that the woman would push in beside his mother. He could think of no better arrangement.

As she waited for her tokens, the woman was surveying the seating possibilities — he hoped with the idea of sitting where she was least wanted. There was something familiar-looking about her but Julian could not place what it was. She was a giant of a woman. Her face was set not only to meet opposition but to seek it out. The downward tilt of her large lower lip was like a warning sign: DON'T TAMPER WITH ME. Her bulging figure was encased in a green crepe dress and her feet overflowed in red shoes. She had on a hideous hat. A purple velvet flap came down on one side of it and stood up on the other; the rest of it was green and looked like a cushion with the stuffing out. She carried a mammoth red pocketbook that bulged through-out as if it were stuffed with rocks.

To Julian's disappointment, the little boy climbed up on the empty seat beside his mother. His mother lumped all children, black and white, into the common category, "cute," and she thought little Negroes were on the whole cuter than little white children. She smiled at the little boy as he climbed on the seat.

Meanwhile the woman was bearing down upon the empty seat beside Julian. To his annoyance, she squeezed herself into it. He saw his mother's face change as the woman settled herself next to him and he realized with satisfaction that this was more objectionable to her than it was to him. Her face seemed almost gray and there was a look of dull recognition in her eyes, as if suddenly she had sickened at some awful confrontation. Julian saw that it was because she and the woman had, in a sense, swapped sons. Though his mother would not realize the symbolic significance of this, she would feel it. His amusement showed plainly on his face.

The woman next to him muttered something unintelligible to herself. He was conscious of a kind of bristling next to him, a muted growling like that of an angry cat. He could not see anything but the red pocketbook upright on the bulging green thighs. He visualized the woman as she had stood waiting for her tokens — the ponderous figure, rising from the red shoes upward over the solid hips, the mammoth bosom, the haughty face, the green and purple hat.

His eyes widened.

The vision of the two hats, identical, broke upon him with the radiance of a brilliant sunrise. His face was suddenly lit with joy. He could not believe that Fate had thrust upon his mother such a lesson. He gave a loud chuckle so that she would look at him and see that he saw. She turned her eyes on him slowly. The blue in them seemed to have turned a bruised purple. For a moment he had an uncomfortable sense of her innocence, but it lasted only a second before principle rescued him. Justice entitled him to laugh. His grin hardened until it said to her as plainly as if he were saying aloud: Your punishment exactly fits your pettiness. This should teach you a permanent lesson.

Her eyes shifted to the woman. She seemed unable to bear looking at him and to find the woman preferable. He became conscious again of the bristling presence at his side. The woman was rumbling like a volcano about to become active. His mother's mouth began to twitch slightly at one corner. With a sinking heart, he saw incipient signs of recovery on her face and realized that this was going to strike her suddenly as funny and was going to be no lesson at all. She kept her eyes on the woman and an amused smile came over her face as if the woman were a monkey that had stolen her hat. The little Negro was looking up at her with large fascinated eyes. He had been trying to attract her attention for some time.

"Carver!" the woman said suddenly. "Come heah!"

When he saw that the spotlight was on him at last, Carver drew his feet up and turned himself toward Julian's mother and giggled.

"Carver!" the woman said. "You heah me? Come heah!"

Carver slid down from the seat but remained squatting with his back against the base of it, his head turned slyly around toward Julian's mother, who was smiling at him. The woman reached a hand across the aisle and snatched him to her. He righted himself and hung backwards on her knees, grinning at Julian's mother. "Isn't he cute?" Julian's mother said to the woman with the protruding teeth.

"I reckon he is," the woman said without conviction.

The Negress yanked him upright but he eased out of her grip and shot across the aisle and scrambled, giggling wildly, onto the seat beside his love.

"I think he likes me," Julian's mother said, and smiled at the woman. It was the smile she used when she was being particularly gracious to an inferior. Julian saw everything lost. The lesson had rolled off her like rain on a roof.

The woman stood up and yanked the little boy off the seat as if she were snatching him from contagion. Julian could feel the rage in her at having no weapon like his mother's smile. She gave the child a sharp slap across his leg. He howled once and then thrust his head into her stomach and kicked his feet against her shins. "Be-have," she said vehemently.

The bus stopped and the Negro who had been reading the newspaper got off. The woman moved over and set the little boy down with a thump between herself and Julian. She held him firmly by the knee. In a moment he put his hands in front of his face and peeped at Julian's mother through his fingers.

"I see yoooooooo!" she said and put her hand in front of her face and peeped at him.

The woman slapped his hand down. "Quit yo' foolishness," she said, "before I knock the living Jesus out of you!"

Julian was thankful that the next stop was theirs. He reached up and pulled the cord. The woman reached up and pulled it at the same time. Oh my God, he thought. He had the terrible intuition that when they got off the bus together, his mother would open her purse and give the little boy a nickel. The gesture would be as natural to her as breathing. The bus stopped and the woman got up and lunged to the front, dragging the child, who wished to stay on, after her. Julian and his mother got up and followed. As they neared the door, Julian tried to relieve her of her pocketbook.

"No," she murmured, "I want to give the little boy a nickel."

"No!" Julian hissed. "No!"

She smiled down at the child and opened her bag. The bus door opened and the woman picked him up by the arm and descended with him, hanging at her hip. Once in the street she set him down and shook him.

Julian's mother had to close her purse while she got down the bus step but as soon as her feet were on the ground, she opened it again and began to rummage inside. "I can't find but a penny," she whispered, "but it looks like a new one."

"Don't do it!" Julian said fiercely between his teeth. There was a streetlight on the corner and she hurried to get under it so that she could better see into her pocketbook. The woman was heading off rapidly down the street with the child still hanging backward on her hand.

"Oh little boy!" Julian's mother called and took a few quick steps and caught up with them just beyond the lamppost. "Here's a bright new penny for you," and she held out the coin which shone bronze in the dim light.

The huge woman turned and for a moment stood, her shoulders lifted and her face frozen with frustrated rage, and stared at Julian's mother. Then all at once she seemed to explode like a piece of machinery that had been given one ounce of pressure too much. Julian saw the black fist swing out with the red pocketbook. He shut his eyes and cringed as he heard the woman shout, "He don't take nobody's pennies!" When he opened his eyes, the woman was disappearing down the street with the little boy staring wide-eyed over her shoulder. Julian's mother was sitting on the sidewalk.

"I told you not to do that," Julian said angrily. "I told you not to do that!"

He stood over her for a minute, gritting his teeth. Her legs were stretched out in front of her and her hat was on her lap. He squatted down and looked her in the face. It was totally expressionless. "You got exactly what you deserved," he said. "Now get up."

He picked up her pocketbook and put what had fallen out back in it. He picked the hat up off her lap. The penny caught his eye on the sidewalk and he picked that up and let it drop before her eyes into the purse. Then he stood up and leaned over and held his hands out to pull her up. She remained immobile. He sighed. Rising above them on either side were black apartment buildings, marked with irregular rectangles of light. At the end of the block a man came out of a door and walked off in the opposite direction. "All right," he said, "suppose somebody happens by and wants to know why you're sitting on the sidewalk?"

She took the hand and, breathing hard, pulled heavily up on it and then stood for a moment, swaying slightly as if the spots of light in the darkness were circling around her. Her eyes, shadowed and confused, finally settled on his face. He did not try to conceal his irritation. "I hope this teaches you a lesson," he said. She leaned forward and her eyes raked his face. She seemed trying to determine his identity. Then, as if she found nothing familiar about him, she started off with a headlong movement in the wrong direction.

"Aren't you going on to the Y?" he asked.

"Home," she muttered.

"Well, are we walking?"

For answer she kept going. Julian followed along, his hands behind him. He saw no reason to let the lesson she had had go without backing it up with an explanation of its meaning. She might as well be made to understand what had happened to her. "Don't think that was just an uppity Negro woman," he said. "That was the whole colored race which will no longer take your condescending pennies. That was your black double. She can wear the same hat as you, and to be sure," he added gratuitously (because he thought it was funny), "it looked better on her than it did on you. What all this means," he said, "is that the old world is gone. The old manners are obsolete and your graciousness is not worth a damn." He thought bitterly of the house that had been lost for him. "You aren't who you think you are," he said.

She continued to plow ahead, paying no attention to him. Her hair had come undone on one side. She dropped her pocketbook and took no notice. He stooped and picked it up and handed it to her but she did not take it.

"You needn't act as if the world had come to an end," he said, " because it hasn't. From now on you've got to live in a new world and face a few realities for a change. Buck up," he said, "it won't kill you."

She was breathing fast.

"Let's wait on the bus," he said.

"Home," she said thickly.

"I hate to see you behave like this," he said. " Just like a child. I should be able to expect more of you." He decided to stop where he was and make her stop and wait for a bus. " I'm not going any farther," he said, stopping. "We're going on the bus."

She continued to go on as if she had not heard him. He took a few steps and caught her arm and stopped her. He looked into her face and caught his breath. He was looking into a face he had never seen before. "Tell Grandpa to come get me," she said.

He stared, stricken.

"Tell Caroline to come get me," she said.

Stunned, he let her go and she lurched forward again, walking as if one leg were shorter than the other. A tide of darkness seemed to be sweeping her from him. "Mother!" he cried. "Darling, sweetheart, wait!" Crumpling,

she fell to the pavement. He dashed forward and fell at her side, crying, "Mamma, Mamma!" He turned her over. Her face was fiercely distorted. One eye, large and staring, moved slightly to the left as if it had become unmoored. The other remained fixed on him, raked his face again, found
5 nothing and closed.
"Wait here, wait here!" he cried and jumped up and began to run for help toward a cluster of lights he saw in the distance ahead of him. "Help, help!" he shouted, but his voice was thin, scarcely a thread of sound. The lights drifted farther away the faster he ran and his feet moved numbly as if they
10 carried him nowhere. The tide of darkness seemed to sweep him back to her, postponing from moment to moment his entry into the world of guilt and sorrow.

Biographical Notes

Flannery O'Connor was born in Savannah, Georgia, in 1925. She wrote two novels, Wise Blood *(1952) and* The Violent Bear It Away *(1960), as well as 31 short stories. She died in 1964 after having long suffered from a rare blood disease. When once asked what had been the major influences on her life, she answered, "Probably being a Catholic, and a Southerner".*

"Everything That Rises Must Converge" was first published in New World Writing *and later included in her collection of short stories bearing the same title.*

Annotations

13 3 **reducing class** course where one learns how to lose weight – **Y** *short for:* YWCA (Young Women's Christian Association) – 7 **to integrate** *here:* to give blacks and whites equal rights in the use of transportation facilities – 11 **to brace o.s.** to make o.s. ready for s.th. unpleasant – 13 **pinned** fastened – 14 **Saint Sebastian** a Roman martyr who was killed by arrows – 19 **hideous** ['hɪdɪəs] extremely ugly – **flap** a flat thin part that hangs down – 21 **stuffing** soft material used to fill cushions – 22 **jaunty** *here:* smart – **pathetic** arousing pity – 25 **to protrude** to stick out – **florid** having a red skin – 32 **walk** path leading up to the house – 33 **bulbous** shaped like a bulb

14 4 **grubby** dirty – 6 **to glaze** *here:* to become glassy and lifeless – **numb** [nʌm] without feeling, indifferent – 8 **dumpy** short and fat – **surmounted by** with the … on top – 9 **atrocious** [əˈtrəʊʃəs] *here:* very ugly – 10 **I won't meet myself coming and going** I will be the only person wearing such a hat – 12 **gloomily** with a feeling of depression – 13 **whenever you take the fit** whenever you feel like it – 14 **to visualize** [ˈvɪʒʊəlaɪz] to form a mental image of – 28 **hag** ugly old woman – 29 **saturated** completely filled with – **martyrdom** great suffering – 31 **to wait on** *dial.* to wait for – 35 **vicious** [ˈvɪʃəs] cruel

15 4 **gracious** [ˈgreɪʃəs] polite, kind and generous – 17 **jerkily** with sudden stops and starts – 18 **dingy** [ˈdɪndʒɪ] dirty and shabby – 22 **to groan** to make a deep sound expressing despair – 28 **let's skip it** let's drop the subject – 40 **mortgage** [mɔːrgɪdʒ] money borrowed from a bank against the security of a house

16 3 **decayed mansion** large house in a bad state of repair – 8 **rustle** soft, light sound as of dry leaves – 10 **faded** having lost their color – **draperies** long heavy curtains – 12 **threadbare** shabby – 16 **darky** *coll.* discriminatory term for a black American – 23 **to lay off** *coll.* to stop criticizing – 24 **vile** evil – 27 **to scowl** [aʊ] to look angrily – 30 **it was borne in upon him** he was forced to take notice of it – 31 **bleakly** in a discouraging manner – **preposterous** [-ˈ- - -] absurd – 39 **thug** violent criminal

17 12 **to hoist** to lift with some effort – 13 **drawing room** room in which guests are received – 14 **token** a piece of stamped metal used for the payment of bus fares – 15 **aisle** [aɪl] narrow passage between rows of seats – 18 **canvas** strong cloth – 22 **fan** device meant to make a flow of air by waving it – 24 **I reckon it might could** *substandard English:* I reckon it might – 28 **to cringe** *here:* to shrink in disgust – 30 **they were thick as fleas** *here:* the bus was full of them (blacks) – 33 **fix** *coll.* situation from which it is difficult to escape – 34 **to get one's goat** *coll.* to annoy s.o., to anger s.o. – 37 **reformatory** [-ˈ- - - -] institution to which young people convicted of minor crimes are sent

18 3 **to peer** to look closely – 4 **malevolent** [-ˈ- - -] wishing to do evil to others – **to subside** to sink – 19 **premise** [ˈpremɪs] *here:* assumption – 32 **had gone unfilled** had not been repaired by the dentist – 38 **to be disenchanted** to be disillusioned

19 8 **to lurch** to move with a sudden change of weight – 9 **to right oneself** to bring oneself back to the normal position – 24 **serenely** [sɪˈriːnlɪ] calmly – 30 **entrenched behind** protected by – 33 **reproachfully** finding fault with – 34 **avidly** in an eager way

20 1 **to deter** to prevent s.o. from doing s.th. – 6 **battered** *fig.* beaten – 13 **stolidly** not showing any feeling – 26 **to shrivel** to lose freshness – 27 **pump** low-cut shoe without a fastening – 28 **to train a look on** to direct one's eyes towards – 29 **detached** separated – 31 **obnoxious** [əbˈnɒkʃəs] very unpleasant, nasty – 36 **stroke** sudden illness with loss of feeling, power to move, etc. (Schlaganfall) – 37 **to strike up** to begin – 40 **sonorous** [sɒnərəs] having a full deep sound – **solemnity** formality, seriousness

21 1 **undertaker** manager of burials and funerals – 2 **stilted** stiff and unnatural – 8 **to linger** to stay – 9 **ultimate** greatest possible – 10 **suspiciously** *here:* giving a reason to suspect (i.e. that she was a Negro) – 12 **dignified** worthy – 13 **to persecute** to treat cruelly – 16 **dwarf-like** as a person of much less than the usual size – 17 **mummy** well-preserved dead body – 18 **to be tilted** *here:* to be thrown (forward) – 19 **sullen** silently

showing dislike or bad temper – 21 **plaid** [æ] cloth with a pattern of squares – 29 **tilt** *here:* slope – 30 **to tamper with** to interfere with – **to bulge** to swell outward – **encased in** completely covered or surrounded with – 34 **pocketbook** *B.E.:* purse – 37 **to lump** *here:* to label, to group

22   1 **to bear down upon** to approach in a threatening manner – 7 **to swap** [ɒ] *coll.* to exchange – 10 **unintelligible** incomprehensible – 11 **bristling** stiffening with fear or anger – **muted** softened or deadened (of a sound) – 14 **ponderous** very heavy, weighty – 15 **mammoth** enormous – **haughty** [ˈhɔːtɪ] proud, arrogant – 22 **bruised** *here:* discolored – 26 **pettiness** insignificance, worthlessness – 32 **incipient** just beginning

23   2 **to squat** [ɒ] to sit on the heels with the knees bent – 9 **to yank** to push or pull with a sharp movement – 10 **to scramble** to climb or crawl on hands and feet – 16 **contagion** [kənˈteɪdʒən] bad influence spread by close contact – 19 **shin** front part of the leg between the knee and the ankle – 34 **to lunge** to move forward suddenly

24   5 **to rummage** to search thoroughly by turning things over – 23 **to grit one's teeth** *fig.* to show courage or determination in a difficult situation – 40 **to rake** to search carefully

25   10 **uppity** *coll.* arrogant, snobbish – 12 **to condescend** [ˌ--ˈ-] to lower oneself – 13 **gratuitously** [grəˈtjuːɪtəslɪ] unnecessarily, done without good reason – 24 **buck up** be more cheerful

26   4 **unmoored** loose, unattached (usually of a boat)

John Cheever

The Enormous Radio

Jim and Irene Westcott were the kind of people who seem to strike that satisfactory average of income, endeavor, and respectability that is reached by the statistical reports in college alumni bulletins. They were the parents of two young children, they had been married nine years, they lived on the twelfth floor of an apartment house near Sutton Place, they went to the theatre on an average of 10.3 times a year, and they hoped someday to live in Westchester. Irene Westcott was a pleasant, rather plain girl with soft brown hair and a wide, fine forehead upon which nothing at all had been written, and in the cold weather she wore a coat of fitch skins dyed to resemble mink. You could not say that Jim Westcott looked younger than he was, but you could at least say of him that he seemed to feel younger. He wore his graying hair cut very short, he dressed in the kind of clothes his class had worn at Andover, and his manner was earnest, vehement, and intentionally naïve. The Westcotts differed from their friends, their classmates, and their neighbors only in an interest they shared in serious music. They went to a great many concerts — although they seldom mentioned this to anyone — and they spent a good deal of time listening to music on the radio.

Their radio was an old instrument, sensitive, unpredictable, and beyond repair. Neither of them understood the mechanics of radio — or of any of the other appliances that surrounded them — and when the instrument faltered, Jim would strike the side of the cabinet with his hand. This sometimes helped. One Sunday afternoon, in the middle of a Schubert quartet, the music faded away altogether. Jim struck the cabinet repeatedly, but there was no response; the Schubert was lost to them forever. He promised to buy Irene a new radio, and on Monday when he came home from work he told her that he had got one. He refused to describe it, and said it would be a surprise for her when it came.

The radio was delivered at the kitchen door the following afternoon, and with the assistance of her maid and the handyman Irene uncrated it and brought it into the living room. She was struck at once with the physical ugliness of the large gumwood cabinet. Irene was proud of her living room, she had chosen its furnishings and colors as carefully as she chose her clothes, and now it seemed to her that the new radio stood among her intimate possessions like an aggressive intruder. She was confounded by the number of dials and switches on the instrument panel, and she studied them thoroughly before she put the plug into a wall socket and turned the radio on. The dials flooded with a malevolent green light, and in the distance she heard the music of a piano quintet. The quintet was in the distance for only an instant; it bore down upon her with a speed greater than light and filled the apartment with the noise of music amplified so mightily that it knocked a china ornament from a table to the floor. She rushed to the instrument and reduced the volume. The violent forces that were snared in the ugly gumwood cabinet made her uneasy. Her children came home from school then, and she took them to the Park. It was not until later in the afternoon that she was able to return to the radio.

    The maid had given the children their suppers and was supervising their baths when Irene turned on the radio, reduced the volume, and sat down to listen to a Mozart quintet that she knew and enjoyed. The music came through clearly. The new instrument had a much purer tone, she thought, than the old one. She decided that tone was most important and that she could conceal the cabinet behind a sofa. But as soon as she had made her peace with the radio, the interference began. A crackling sound like the noise of a burning powder fuse began to accompany the singing of the strings. Beyond the music, there was a rustling that reminded Irene unpleasantly of the sea, and as the quintet progressed, these noises were joined by many others. She tried all the dials and switches but nothing dimmed the interference, and she sat down, disappointed and bewildered, and tried to trace the flight of the melody. The elevator shaft in her building ran beside the living-room wall, and it was the noise of the elevator that gave her a clue to the character of the static. The rattling of the elevator cables and the opening and closing of the elevator doors were reproduced in her loudspeaker, and, realizing that the radio was sensitive to electrical currents of all sorts, she began to discern through the Mozart the ringing of telephone bells, the dialing of phones, and the lamentation of a vacuum cleaner. By listening more carefully, she was able to distinguish doorbells, elevator bells, electric razors, and Waring mixers, whose sounds had been picked up from the apartments that surrounded hers and transmitted through her loudspeaker. The powerful and ugly instrument, with its mistaken sensitivity to discord, was more than she could hope to master, so she turned the thing off and went into the nursery to see her children.

    When Jim Westcott came home that night, he went to the radio confidently and worked the controls. He had the same sort of experience Irene had had. A man was speaking on the station Jim had chosen, and his voice swung instantly from the distance into a force so powerful that it shook the apartment. Jim turned the volume control and reduced the voice. Then, a minute or two later, the interference began. The ringing of telephones and doorbells set in, joined by the rasp of the elevator doors and the whir of cooking appliances. The character of the noice had changed since Irene had tried the radio earlier; the last of the electric razors was being unplugged, the vacuum cleaners had all been returned to their closets, and the static reflected that change in pace that overtakes the city after the sun goes down. He fiddled with the knobs but couldn't get rid of the noises, so he turned the radio off and told Irene that in the morning he'd call the people who had sold it to him and give them hell.

The following afternoon, when Irene returned to the apartment from a luncheon date, the maid told her that a man had come and fixed the radio. Irene went into the living room before she took off her hat or her furs and tried the instrument. From the loudspeaker came a recording of the "Missouri Waltz." It reminded her of the thin, scratchy music from an old-fashioned phonograph that she sometimes heard across the lake where she spent her summers. She waited until the waltz had finished, expecting an explanation of the recording, but there was none. The music was followed by silence, and then the plaintive and scratchy record was repeated. She turned the dial and got a satisfactory burst of Caucasian music — the thump of bare feet in the dust and the rattle of coin jewelry — but in the background she could hear the ringing of bells and a confusion of voices. Her children came home from school then, and she turned off the radio and went to the nursery.

When Jim came home that night, he was tired, and he took a bath and changed his clothes. Then he joined Irene in the living room. He had just turned on the radio when the maid announced dinner, so he left it on, and he and Irene went to the table.

Jim was too tired to make even a pretense of sociability, and there was nothing about the dinner to hold Irene's interest, so her attention wandered from the food to the deposits of silver polish on the candlesticks and from there to the music in the other room. She listened for a few minutes to a Chopin prelude and then was surprised to hear a man's voice break in. "For Christ's sake, Kathy," he said, "do you always have to play the piano when I get home?" The music stopped abruptly. "It's the only chance I have," a woman said. "I'm at the office all day." "So am I," the man said. He added something obscene about an upright piano, and slammed a door. The passionate and melancholy music began again.

"Did you hear that?" Irene asked.

"What?" Jim was eating his dessert.

"The radio. A man said something while the music was still going on — something dirty."

"It's probably a play."

"I don't think it *is* a play," Irene said.

They left the table and took their coffee into the living room. Irene asked Jim to try another station. He turned the knob. "Have you seen my garters?" a man asked. "Button me up," a woman said. "Have you seen my garters?" the man said again. "Just button me up and I'll find your garters," the woman said. Jim shifted to another station. "I wish you wouldn't leave apple cores in the ashtrays," a man said. "I hate the smell."

"This is strange," Jim said.

"Isn't it?" Irene said.

Jim turned the knob again. " 'On the coast of Coromandel where the early pumpkins blow,' " a woman with a pronounced English accent said, " 'in the middle of the woods lived the Yonghy-Bonghy-Bò. Two old chairs, and half a candle, one old jug without a handle . . .' "

"My God!" Irene cried. "That's the Sweeneys' nurse."

" 'These were all his worldly goods,' " the British voice continued.

"Turn that thing off," Irene said. "Maybe they can hear *us*." Jim switched the radio off. "That was Miss Armstrong, the Sweeneys' nurse," Irene said. "She must be reading to the little girl. They live in 17-B. I've talked with Miss Armstrong in the Park. I know her voice very well. We must be getting other people's apartments."

"That's impossible," Jim said.

"Well, that was the Sweeneys' nurse," Irene said hotly. "I know her voice. I know it very well. I'm wondering if they can hear us."

Jim turned the switch. First from a distance and then nearer, nearer, as if borne on the wind, came the pure accents of the Sweeneys' nurse again: " '*Lady Jingly! Lady Jingly!*' " she said, " '*sitting where the pumpkins blow, will you come and be my wife?* said the Yonghy-Bonghy-Bò . . .' "

Jim went over to the radio and said "Hello" loudly into the speaker.

" '*I am tired of living singly*,' " the nurse went on, " '*on this coast so wild and shingly, I'm a-weary of my life; if you'll come and be my wife, quite serene would be my life . . .*' "

"I guess she can't hear us," Irene said. "Try something else."

Jim turned to another station, and the living room was filled with the uproar of a cocktail party that had overshot its mark. Someone was playing the piano and singing the "Whiffenpoof Song", and the voices that surrounded the piano were vehement and happy. "Eat some more sandwiches," a woman shrieked. There were screams of laughter and a dish of some sort crashed to the floor.

"Those must be the Fullers, in 11-E," Irene said. "I knew they were giving a party this afternoon. I saw her in the liquor store. Isn't this too divine? Try something else. See if you can get those people in 18-C."

The Westcotts overheard that evening a monologue on salmon fishing in Canada, a bridge game, running comments on home movies of what had apparently been a fortnight at Sea Island, and a bitter family quarrel about an overdraft at the bank. They turned off their radio at midnight and went to bed, weak with laughter. Sometime in the night, their son began to call for a glass of water and Irene got one and took it to his room. It was very early. All the lights in the neighborhood were extinguished, and from the boy's window she could see the empty street. She went into the living room and tried the radio. There was some faint coughing, a moan, and then a man spoke. "Are you all right, darling?" he asked. "Yes," a woman said wearily. "Yes, I'm all right, I guess," and then she added with great feeling. "But, you know, Charlie, I don't feel like myself any more. Sometimes there are about fifteen or twenty minutes in the week when I feel like myself. I don't like to go to another doctor, because the doctor's bills are so awful already, but I just don't feel like myself, Charlie. I just never feel like myself." They were not young, Irene thought. She guessed from the timbre of their voices that they were middle-aged. The restrained melancholy of the dialogue and the draft from the bedroom window made her shiver, and she went back to bed.

The following morning, Irene cooked breakfast for the family — the maid didn't come up from her room in the basement until ten — braided her daughter's hair, and waited at the door until her children and her husband had been carried away in the elevator. Then she went into the living room and tried the radio. "I don't want to go to school," a child screamed. "I hate school. I won't go to school. I hate school." "You will go to school," an enraged woman said. "We paid eight hundred dollars to get you into that school and you'll go if it kills you." The next number on the dial produced the worn record of the "Missouri Waltz." Irene shifted the control and invaded the privacy of several breakfast tables. She overheard demonstrations of indigestion, carnal love, abysmal vanity, faith, and despair. Irene's life was nearly as simple and sheltered as it appeared to be, and the forthright and sometimes brutal language that came from the loudspeaker that morning astonished and troubled her. She continued to listen until her maid came in. Then she turned off the radio quickly, since this insight, she realized, was a furtive one.

Irene had a luncheon date with a friend that day, and she left her apartment at a little after twelve. There were a number of women in the elevator when it stopped at her floor. She stared at their handsome and impassive faces, their furs, and the cloth flowers in their hats. Which one of them had been to Sea Island? she wondered. Which one had overdrawn her bank account? The elevator stopped at the tenth floor and a woman with a pair of Skye terriers joined them. Her hair was rigged high on her head and she wore a mink cape. She was humming the "Missouri Waltz."

Irene had two Martinis at lunch, and she looked searchingly at her friend and wondered what her secrets were. They had intended to go shopping after lunch, but Irene excused herself and went home. She told the maid that she was not to be disturbed; then she went into the living room, closed the doors, and switched on the radio. She heard, in the course of the afternoon, the halting conversation of a woman entertaining her aunt, the hysterical conclusion of a luncheon party, and a hostess briefing her maid about some cocktail guests. "Don't give the best Scotch to anyone who hasn't white hair," the hostess said. "See if you can get rid of that liver paste before you pass those hot things, and could you lend me five dollars? I want to tip the elevator man."

As the afternoon waned, the conversations increased in intensity. From where Irene sat, she could see the open sky above the East River. There were hundreds of clouds in the sky, as though the south wind had broken the winter into pieces and were blowing it north, and on her radio she could hear the arrival of cocktail guests and the return of children and businessmen from their schools and offices. "I found a good-sized diamond on the bathroom floor this morning," a woman said. "It must have fallen out of that bracelet Mrs. Dunston was wearing last night." "We'll sell it," a man said. "Take it down to the jeweler on Madison Avenue and sell it. Mrs. Dunston won't know the difference, and we could use a couple of hundred bucks ..." "'Oranges and lemons, say the bells of St. Clement's,'" the Sweeneys' nurse sang. "'Halfpence and farthings, say the bells of St. Martin's. When will you pay me? say the bells at old Bailey ...'" "It's not a hat," a woman cried, and at her back roared a cocktail party. "It's not a hat, it's a love affair. That's what Walter Florell said. He said it's not a hat, it's a love affair," and then, in a lower voice, the same woman added, "Talk to somebody, for Christ's sake, honey, talk to somebody. If she catches you standing here not talking to anybody, she'll take us off her invitation list, and I love these parties."

The Westcotts were going out for dinner that night, and when Jim came home, Irene was dressing. She seemed sad and vague, and he brought her a drink. They were dining with friends in the neighborhood, and they walked to where they were going. The sky was broad and filled with light. It was one of those splendid evenings that excite memory and desire, and the air that touched their hands and faces felt very soft. A Salvation Army band was on the corner playing "Jesus Is Sweeter." Irene drew on her husband's arm and held him there for a minute, to hear the music. "They're really such nice people, aren't they?" she said. "They have such nice faces. Actually, they're so much nicer than a lot of the people we know." She took a bill from her purse and walked over and dropped it into the tambourine. There was in her face, when she returned to her husband, a look of radiant melancholy that he was not familiar with. And her conduct at the dinner party that night seemed strange to him, too. She interrupted her hostess rudely and stared at the people across the table from her with an intensity for which she would have punished her children.

It was still mild when they walked home from the party, and Irene looked up at the spring stars. "'How far that little candle throws its beams,'" she exclaimed. "'So shines a good deed in a naughty world.'" She waited that night until Jim had fallen asleep, and then went into the living room and turned on the radio.

Jim came home at about six the next night. Emma, the maid, let him in, and he had taken off his hat and was taking off his coat when Irene ran into the hall. Her face was shining with tears and her hair was disordered. "Go up to 16-C, Jim!" she screamed. "Don't take off your coat. Go up to 16-C. Mr. Osborn's beating his wife. They've been quarreling since four o'clock, and now he's hitting her. Go up there and stop him."

From the radio in the living room, Jim heard screams, obscenities, and thuds. "You know you don't have to listen to this sort of thing," he said. He strode into the living room and turned the switch. "It's indecent," he said. "It's like looking in windows. You know you don't have to listen to this sort of thing. You can turn it off."

"Oh, it's so horrible, it's so dreadful," Irene was sobbing. "I've been listening all day, and it's so depressing."

"Well, if it's so depressing, why do you listen to it? I bought this damned radio to give you some pleasure," he said. "I paid a great deal of money for it. I thought it might make you happy. I wanted to make you happy."

"Don't, don't, don't, don't quarrel with me," she moaned, and laid her head on his shoulder. "All the others have been quarreling all day. Everybody's been quarreling. They're all worried about money. Mrs. Hutchinson's mother is dying of cancer in Florida and they don't have enough money to send her to the Mayo Clinic. At least, Mr. Hutchinson says they don't have enough money. And some woman in this building is having an affair with the handyman — with that hideous handyman. It's too disgusting. And Mrs. Melville has heart trouble and Mr. Hendricks is going to lose his job in April and Mrs. Hendricks is horrid about the whole thing and that girl who plays the 'Missouri Waltz' is a whore, a common whore, and the elevator man has tuberculosis and Mr. Osborn has been beating Mrs. Osborn." She wailed, she trembled with grief and checked the stream of tears down her face with the heel of her palm.

"Well, why do you have to listen?" Jim asked again. "Why do you have to listen to this stuff if it makes you so miserable?"

"Oh, don't, don't, don't," she cried. "Life is too terrible, too sordid and awful. But we've never been like that, have we, darling? Have we? I mean, we've always been good and decent and loving to one another, haven't we? And we have two children, two beautiful children. Our lives aren't sordid, are they, darling? Are they?" She flung her arms around his neck and drew his face down to hers. "We're happy, aren't we, darling? We are happy, aren't we?"

"Of course we're happy," he said tiredly. He began to surrender his resentment. "Of course we're happy. I'll have that damned radio fixed or taken away tomorrow." He stroked her soft hair. "My poor girl," he said.

"You love me, don't you?" she asked. "And we're not hypercritical or worried about money or dishonest, are we?"

"No, darling," he said.

A man came in the morning and fixed the radio. Irene turned it on cautiously and was happy to hear a California-wine commercial and a recording of Beethoven's Ninth Symphony, including Schiller's "Ode to Joy." She kept the radio on all day and nothing untoward came from the speaker.

A Spanish suite was being played when Jim came home. "Is everything all right?" he asked. His face was pale, she thought. They had some cocktails and went in to dinner to the "Anvil Chorus" from *Il Trovatore*. This was followed by Debussy's "La Mer."

"I paid the bill for the radio today," Jim said. "It cost four hundred dollars. I hope you'll get some enjoyment out of it."

"Oh, I'm sure I will," Irene said.

"Four hundred dollars is a good deal more than I can afford," he went on. "I wanted to get something that you'd enjoy. It's the last extravagance we'll be able to indulge in this year. I see that you haven't paid your clothing bills yet. I saw them on your dressing table." He looked directly at her. "Why did you tell me you'd paid them? Why did you lie to me?"

"I just didn't want you to worry, Jim," she said. She drank some water. "I'll be able to pay my bills out of this month's allowance. There were the slipcovers last month, and that party."

"You've got to learn to handle the money I give you a little more intelligently, Irene," he said. "You've got to understand that we don't have as much money this year as we had last. I had a very sobering talk with Mitchell today. No one is buying anything. We're spending all our time promoting new issues, and you know how long that takes. I'm not getting any younger, you know. I'm thirty-seven. My hair will be gray next year. I haven't done as well as I'd hoped to do. And I don't suppose things will get any better."

"Yes, dear," she said.

"We've got to start cutting down," Jim said. "We've got to think of the children. To be perfectly frank with you, I worry about money a great deal. I'm not at all sure of the future. No one is. If anything should happen to me, there's the insurance, but that wouldn't go very far today. I've worked awfully hard to give you and the children a comfortable life," he said bitterly. "I don't like to see all my energies, all of my youth, wasted in fur coats and radios and slipcovers and —"

"Please, Jim," she said. "Please. They'll hear us."

"*Who'll hear us?* Emma can't hear us."

"The radio."

"Oh, I'm sick!" he shouted. "I'm sick to death of your apprehensiveness. The radio can't hear us. Nobody can hear us. And what if they can hear us? Who cares?"

Irene got up from the table and went into the living room. Jim went to the door and shouted at her from there. "Why are you so Christly all of a sudden? What's turned you overnight into a convent girl? You stole your mother's jewelry before they probated her will. You never gave your sister a cent of that money that was intended for her — not even when she needed it. You made Grace Howland's life miserable, and where was all your piety and your virtue when you went to that abortionist? I'll never forget how cool you were. You packed your bag and went off to have that child murdered as if you were going to Nassau. If you'd had any reasons, if you'd had any good reasons —"

Irene stood for a minute before the hideous cabinet, disgraced and sickened, but she held her hand on the switch before she extinguished the music

and the voices, hoping that the instrument might speak to her kindly, that she might hear the Sweeneys' nurse. Jim continued to shout at her from the door. The voice on the radio was suave and noncommital. "An early-morning railroad disaster in Tokyo," the loudspeaker said, "killed twenty-nine
5 people. A fire in a Catholic hospital near Buffalo for the care of blind children was extinguished early this morning by nuns. The temperature is forty-seven. The humidity is eighty-nine."

Biographical Notes

John Cheever (1912—1982) was born in Quincy, Massachusetts. His first volume of short stories, The Way Some People Live, *appeared in 1942. Its title captures the characteristic feature of Cheever's writing, namely that he is primarily concerned with incidents in the lives of ordinary men and women in everyday situations. In 1978 his collected stories were published under the title* The Stories of John Cheever. *For this volume he was awarded The Pulitzer Prize in 1979.*

His novel The Wapshot Chronicle *(1957) received a National Book Award. This novel about a New England family and its sequel,* The Wapshot Scandal *(1964), reached a very large audience. Cheever wrote two more novels,* Bullet Park *(1969) and* Falconer *(1976).*

"The Enormous Radio" was published in 1953 in a collection of stories bearing the same title. An earlier version of the story had appeared in The New Yorker *in 1947.*

Annotations

29 1 **to strike** *here:* to arrive at – 2 **endeavor** effort – 3 **alumni bulletin** [əˈlʌmnaɪ] regular publication of news about former students – 7 **Westchester** county north of New York City where wealthy people live – 9 **fitch** a European wild cat (Iltis) – **dyed** colored – 10 **mink** a weasel-like animal (Nerz) – 13 **Andover** the name of Jim Westcott's college – 19 **unpredictable** *here:* unreliable – 21 **appliance** machine, generally electrical, for household use – 22 **to falter** *here:* to transmit weakly or with interruptions – 30 **to uncrate** to lift out of a box – 32 **gumwood** wood of the gumtree found in the Western U.S.A. and Australia – **cabinet** outside case of the radio

30 2 **intruder** person or thing that enters a place without invitation – **confounded** confused – 3 **dial** plate showing different broadcasting stations – **instrument panel** the part of the radio where the switches are – 4 **wall socket** the place in a wall where you can put a plug in order to make an electrical connection – 5 **malevolent** [mə'levələnt] nasty, evil – 7 **to bear down on** to move quickly towards – 8 **to amplify** to increase the strength of – 10 **to snare** to trap – 14 **to supervise** to watch and direct (an activity) – 20 **interference** [ˌɪntə'fɪərəns] *here:* unwanted sounds – **to crackle** to make a number of small cracking sounds as when dry twigs are broken – 21 **powder fuse** narrow tube filled with material which burns and then sets off an explosion – 22 **strings** musical instruments such as violins – **rustling** ['rʌslɪŋ] gentle, light sounds such as made by dry leaves blown by the wind – 24 **to dim** to reduce, to lessen – 25 **bewildered** confused – 26 **to trace** to discover – 31 **to discern** to recognize – 32 **lamentation** *here:* sad sound – 34 **Waring** [eə] name of a manufacturer of mixers – 37 **discord** lack of harmony between sounds – 40 **controls** switches on the instrument panel

31 5 **rasp** rough sound – **whir** [wɜː(r)] sound of s.th. moving or turning quickly – 8 **closet** ['klɒzɪt] cupboard or small room – 9 **pace** speed – 21 **plaintive** sounding sad – 31 **pretense** (*B.E.* pretence) appearing to be or do s.th. – **sociability** *here:* willingness to make conversation

32 10 **garter** elastic material used to keep stockings in place – 12 **core** hard center of a fruit – 15 **Coromandel Coast** a coastal region in south-east India, used by Edward Lear (1812–1888) as the setting for his nonsense poem 'The Courtship of the Yonghy-Bonghy-Bò'. Lear's nonsense poems are still frequently read to British children. – 16 **pumpkin** large orange-yellow fruit (Kürbis) – 24 **the Park** Central Park in New York City – 35 **shingly** covered with small stones – 36 **serene** calm and bright – 39 **to overshoot its mark** to go further than is intended or proper

33 2 **to shriek** [iː] to scream – 6 **divine** *coll.* very pleasing, excellent – 7 **salmon** ['sæmən] large fish with orange-pink flesh – 10 **overdraft** withdrawal of more money than one has in a bank account – 13 **to extinguish** to put out (a light or fire) – 22 **timbre** ['tæmbə(r)] characteristic sound produced by a voice or instrument – 23 **restrained** not emotional, kept under control – 27 **to braid** to twist together into one band – 36 **indigestion** pain from difficulty in absorbing food – **carnal love** sexual intercourse – **abysmal** [–'– –] complete, extreme – **vanity** having too high an opinion of one's looks, abilities, etc. – 37 **to shelter** to protect, to keep safe from danger or unpleasantness – **forthright** direct, going straight to the point

34 2 **furtive** done secretly so as not to attract attention – 5 **impassive** showing no sign of feeling – 9 **Skye terrier** small dog named after the Isle of Skye in Scotland – **to rig** *here:* to pile up – 11 **Martini** a cocktail made of Martini and gin – 16 **halting** hesitating, with breaks – 17 **to brief** to instruct – 22 **to wane** *here:* to go on, to come to an end – 23 **East River** the river separating Manhattan Island and Long Island – 30 **Madison Avenue** a street in New York City with expensive shops and offices – 32 **buck** *coll.* dollar – **Oranges and lemons** a very old nursery rhyme; the names refer to churches in London – 33 **farthing** a quarter of an old British penny; it was used up to 1961

35 12 **radiant** showing great pleasure or joy – 19 **naughty** bad, evil – 29 **thud** sound caused by s.th. heavy striking s.th. soft – 38 **to moan** to speak in a complaining voice

36 5 **hideous** ['hɪdɪəs] frightful, terribly ugly – 8 **whore** [hɔːr] prostitute – 10 **to wail** to cry or complain in a loud voice – 11 **heel** *here:* the place where the palm of the hand and the wrist are joined – 14 **sordid** miserable, full of meanness – 21 **to surrender one's resentment** to stop feeling bitter or angry – 24 **hypercritical** ['haɪpərˌkrɪtɪkl] excessively critical, usually of unimportant things – 30 **untoward** not wanted, unpleasant – 33 **anvil** the large block of iron on which a blacksmith works

37 1 **to indulge in** to allow oneself the pleasure of – 5 **allowance** sum of money given to s.o. – 6 **slipcover** removable cloth covering for a piece of furniture – 9 **sobering** serious; *here:* dealing with unpleasant realities – 11 **to promote new issues** *here:* to put new shares (Aktien) into circulation – 26 **apprehensiveness** anxiety, uneasiness – 30 **Christly** [aɪ] like Jesus Christ – 31 **convent girl** a girl who behaves like a nun – 32 **to probate a will** ['prəʊbeɪt] to establish officially the legality of a testament – 34 **piety** behavior that pleases God – 35 **abortionist** person who illegally stops the growth of an unborn child – 37 **Nassau** ['næsɔː] the capital of the Bahamas, well known as a place for holidays – 39 **disgraced** feeling ashamed

38 3 **suave** [swɑːv] smooth in manner, but possibly not sincere – **noncommittal** not expressing any particular opinion, neutral – 7 **forty-seven** forty-seven degrees Fahrenheit (about 8 degrees Centigrade)

Saul Bellow

A Father-to-Be

The strangest notions had a way of forcing themselves into Rogin's mind. Just thirty-one and passable-looking, with short black hair, small eyes, but a high, open forehead, he was a research chemist, and his mind was generally serious and dependable. But on a snowy Sunday evening while this stocky man, buttoned to the chin in a Burberry coat and walking in his preposterous gait — feet turned outward — was going toward the subway, he fell into a peculiar state.

He was on his way to have supper with his fiancée. She had phoned him a short while ago and said, "You'd better pick up a few things on the way."

"What do we need?"

"Some roast beef, for one thing. I bought a quarter of a pound coming home from my aunt's."

"Why a quarter of a pound, Joan?" said Rogin, deeply annoyed. "That's just about enough for one good sandwich."

"So you have to stop at a delicatessen. I had no more money."

He was about to ask, "What happened to the thirty dollars I gave you on Wednesday?" but he knew that would not be right.

"I had to give Phyllis money for the cleaning woman," said Joan.

Phyllis, Joan's cousin, was a young divorcee, extremely wealthy. The two women shared an apartment.

"Roast beef," he said, "and what else?"

"Some shampoo, sweetheart. We've used up all the shampoo. And hurry, darling, I've missed you all day."

"And I've missed you," said Rogin, but to tell the truth he had been worrying most of the time. He had a younger brother whom he was putting through college. And his mother, whose annuity wasn't quite enough in these days of inflation and high taxes, needed money, too. Joan had debts he was helping her to pay, for she wasn't working. She was looking for something suitable to do. Beautiful, well-educated, aristocratic in her attitude, she couldn't clerk in a dime store; she couldn't model clothes (Rogin thought this made girls vain and stiff, and he didn't want her to); she couldn't be a waitress or a cashier. What could she be? Well, something would turn up and meantime Rogin hesitated to complain. He paid her bills — the dentist, the department store, the osteopath, the doctor, the psychiatrist. At Christmas, Rogin almost went mad. Joan bought him a velvet smoking jacket with frog fasteners, a beautiful pipe, and a pouch. She bought Phyllis a garnet brooch, an Italian silk umbrella, and a gold cigarette holder. For other friends, she bought Dutch pewter and Swedish glassware. Before she was through, she had spent five hundred dollars of Rogin's money. He loved her too much to show his suffering. He believed she had a far better nature than his. She didn't worry about money. She had a marvelous character, always cheerful, and she really didn't need a psychiatrist at all. She went to one because Phyllis did and it made her curious. She tried too much to keep up with her cousin, whose father had made millions in the rug business.

While the woman in the drugstore was wrapping the shampoo bottle, a clear idea suddenly arose in Rogin's thoughts: Money surrounds you in life as the earth does in death. Superimposition is the universal law. Who is free? No one is free. Who has no burdens? Everyone is under pressure. The very rocks, the waters of the earth, beasts, men, children — everyone has some weight to carry. This idea was extremely clear to him at first. Soon it became rather vague, but it had a great effect nevertheless, as if someone had given him a valuable gift. (Not like the velvet smoking jacket he couldn't bring himself to wear, or the pipe it choked him to smoke.) The notion that all were under pressure and affliction, instead of saddening him, had the opposite influence. It put him in a wonderful mood. It was extraordinary how happy he became and, in addition, clear-sighted. His eyes all at once were opened to what was around him. He saw with delight how the druggist and the woman who wrapped the shampoo bottle were smiling and flirting, how the lines of worry in her face went over into lines of cheer and the druggist's receding gums did not hinder his kidding and friendliness. And in the delicatessen, also, it was amazing how much Rogin noted and what happiness it gave him simply to be there.

Delicatessens on Sunday night, when all other stores are shut, will overcharge you ferociously, and Rogin would normally have been on guard, but he was not tonight, or scarcely so. Smells of pickle, sausage, mustard, and smoked fish overjoyed him. He pitied the people who would buy the chicken salad and chopped herring; they could do it only because their sight was too dim to see what they were getting — the fat flakes of pepper on the chicken, the soppy herring, mostly vinegar-soaked stale bread. Who would buy them? Late risers, people living alone, waking up in the darkness of the afternoon, finding their refrigerators empty, or people whose gaze was

turned inward. The roast beef looked not bad, and Rogin ordered a pound. While the storekeeper was slicing the meat, he yelled at a Puerto Rican kid who was reaching for a bag of chocolate cookies. "Hey, you want to pull me down the whole display on yourself? You, *chico*, wait a half a minute."
5 This storekeeper, though he looked like one of Pancho Villa's bandits, the kind that smeared their enemies with syrup and staked them down on anthills, a man with toadlike eyes and stout hands made to clasp pistols hung around his belly, was not so bad. He was a New York man, thought Rogin — who was from Albany himself — a New York man toughened by
10 every abuse of the city, trained to suspect everyone. But in his own realm, on the board behind the counter, there was justice. Even clemency.

The Puerto Rican kid wore a complete cowboy outfit — a green hat with white braid, guns, chaps, spurs, boots, and gauntlets — but he couldn't speak any English. Rogin unhooked the cellophane bag of hard circular
15 cookies and gave it to him. The boy tore the cellophane with his teeth and began to chew one of those dry chocolate disks. Rogin recognized his state — the energetic dream of childhood. Once, he, too, had found these dry biscuits delicious. It would have bored him now to eat one.

What else would Joan like? Rogin thought fondly. Some strawberries.
20 "Give me some frozen strawberries. No, raspberries, she likes those better. And heavy cream. And some rolls, cream cheese, and some of those rubber-looking gherkins."

"What rubber?"

"Those, deep green, with eyes. Some ice cream might be in order, too."
25 He tried to think of a compliment, a good comparison, an endearment, for Joan when she'd open the door. What about her complexion? There was really nothing to compare her sweet, small, daring, shapely, timid, defiant, loving face to. How difficult she was, and how beautiful!

As Rogin went down into the stony, odorous, metallic, captive air of the
30 subway, he was diverted by an unusual confession made by a man to his friend. These were two very tall men, shapeless in their winter clothes, as if their coats concealed suits of chain mail.

"So, how long have you known me?" said one.

"Twelve years."
35 "Well, I have an admission to make," he said. "I've decided that I might as well. For years I've been a heavy drinker. You didn't know. Practically an alcoholic."

But his friend was not surprised, and he answered immediately, "Yes, I did know."
40 "You knew? Impossible! How could you?"

Why, thought Rogin, as if it could be a secret! Look at that long, austere, alcohol-washed face, that drink-ruined nose, the skin by his ears like turkey wattles, and those whisky-saddened eyes.

"Well, I did know, though."

"You couldn't have. I can't believe it." He was upset, and his friend didn't seem to want to soothe him. "But it's all right now," he said. "I've been going to a doctor and taking pills, a new revolutionary Danish discovery. It's a miracle. I'm beginning to believe they can cure you of anything and everything. You can't beat the Danes in science. They do everything. They turned a man into a woman."

"That isn't how they stop you from drinking, is it?"

"No. I hope not. This is only like aspirin. It's superaspirin. They called it the aspirin of the future. But if you use it, you have to stop drinking."

Rogin's illuminated mind asked of itself while the human tides of the subway swayed back and forth, and cars linked and transparent like fish bladders raced under the streets: How come he thought nobody would know what everybody couldn't help knowing? And, as a chemist, he asked himself what kind of compound this new Danish drug might be, and started thinking about various inventions of his own, synthetic albumen, a cigarette that lit itself, a cheaper motor fuel. Ye gods, but he needed money! As never before. What was to be done? His mother was growing more and more difficult. On Friday night, she had neglected to cut up his meat for him, and he was hurt. She had sat at the table motionless, with her long-suffering face, severe, and let him cut his own meat, a thing she almost never did. She had always spoiled him and made his brother envy him. But what she expected now! Oh, Lord, how he had to pay, and it had never even occurred to him formerly that these things might have a price.

Seated, one of the passengers, Rogin recovered his calm, happy, even clairvoyant state of mind. To think of money was to think as the world wanted you to think; then you'd never be your own master. When people said they wouldn't do something for love or money, they meant that love and money were opposite passions and one the enemy of the other. He went on to reflect how little people knew about this, how they slept through life, how small a light the light of consciousness was. Rogin's clean, snub-nosed face shone while his heart was torn with joy at these deeper thoughts of our ignorance. You might take this drunkard as an example, who for long years thought his closest friends never suspected he drank. Rogin looked up and down the aisle for this remarkable knightly symbol, but he was gone.

However, there was no lack of things to see. There was a small girl with a new white muff; into the muff a doll's head was sewn, and the child was happy and affectionately vain of it, while her old man, stout and grim, with a huge scowling nose, kept picking her up and resetting her in the seat, as if he were trying to change her into something else. Then another child, led by her mother, boarded the car, and this other child carried the very same doll-faced muff, and this greatly annoyed both parents. The woman, who looked like a difficult, contentious woman, took her daughter away. It seemed to Rogin that each child was in love with its own muff and didn't even see the other, but it was one of his foibles to think he understood the hearts of little children.

A foreign family next engaged his attention. They looked like Central Americans to him. On one side the mother, quite old, dark-faced, white-haired, and worn out; on the other a son with the whitened, porous hands of a dishwasher. But what was the dwarf who sat between them — a son or a daughter? The hair was long and wavy and the cheeks smooth, but the shirt and tie were masculine. The overcoat was feminine, but the shoes — the shoes were a puzzle. A pair of brown oxfords with an outer seam like a man's, but Baby Louis heels like a woman's — a plain toe like a man's, but a strap across the instep like a woman's. No stockings. That didn't help much. The dwarf's fingers were beringed, but without a wedding band. There were small grim dents in the cheeks. The eyes were puffy and concealed, but Rogin did not doubt that they could reveal strange things if they chose and that this was a creature of remarkable understanding. He had for many years owned de la Mare's *Memoirs of a Midget*. Now he took a resolve; he would read it. As soon as he had decided, he was free from his consuming curiosity as to the dwarf's sex and was able to look at the person who sat beside him.

Thoughts very often grow fertile in the subway, because of the motion, the great company, the subtlety of the rider's state as he rattles under streets and rivers, under the foundations of great buildings, and Rogin's mind had already been strangely stimulated. Clasping the bag of groceries from which there rose odors of bread and pickle spice, he was following a train of reflections, first about the chemistry of sex determination, the X and Y chromosomes, hereditary linkages, the uterus, afterward about his brother as a tax exemption. He recalled two dreams of the night before. In one, an undertaker had offered to cut his hair, and he had refused. In another, he had been carrying a woman on his head. Sad dreams, both! Very sad! Which was the woman — Joan or Mother? And the undertaker — his lawyer? He gave a deep sigh, and by force of habit began to put together his synthetic albumen that was to revolutionize the entire egg industry.

Meanwhile, he had not interrupted his examination of the passengers and had fallen into a study of the man next to him. This was a man whom he had never in his life seen before but with whom he now suddenly felt linked through all existence. He was middle-aged, sturdy, with clear skin and blue eyes. His hands were clean, well formed, but Rogin did not approve of them. The coat he wore was a fairly expensive blue check such as Rogin would never have chosen for himself. He would not have worn blue suède shoes, either, or such a faultless hat, a cumbersome felt animal of a hat encircled by a high, fat ribbon. There are all kinds of dandies, not all of them are of the flaunting kind; some are dandies of respectability, and Rogin's fellow passenger was one of these. His straight-nosed profile was handsome, yet he had betrayed his gift, for he was flat-looking. But in his flat way he seemed to warn people that he wanted no difficulties with them, he wanted nothing to do with them. Wearing such blue suède shoes, he could not afford to have people treading on his feet, and he seemed to draw about himself a circle of privilege, notifying all others to mind their own business and let him read his paper. He was holding a *Tribune*, and perhaps it would be overstatement to say that he was reading. He was holding it.

His clear skin and blue eyes, his straight and purely Roman nose — even the way he sat — all strongly suggested one person to Rogin: Joan. He tried to escape the comparison, but it couldn't be helped. This man not only looked like Joan's father, whom Rogin detested; he looked like Joan herself. Forty years hence, a son of hers, provided she had one, might be like this. A son of hers? Of such a son, he himself, Rogin, would be the father. Lacking in dominant traits as compared with Joan, his heritage would not appear. Probably the children would resemble her. Yes, think forty years ahead, and a man like this, who sat by him knee to knee in the hurtling car among their fellow creatures, unconscious participants in a sort of great carnival of transit — such a man would carry forward what had been Rogin.

This was why he felt bound to him through all existence. What were forty years reckoned against eternity! Forty years were gone, and he was gazing at his own son. Here he was. Rogin was frightened and moved. "My son! My son!" he said to himself, and the pity of it almost made him burst into tears. The holy and frightful work of the masters of life and death brought this about. We were their instruments. We worked toward ends we thought were our own. But no! The whole thing was so unjust. To suffer, to labor, to toil and force your way through the spikes of life, to crawl through its darkest caverns, to push through the worst, to struggle under the weight of economy, to make money — only to become the father of a fourth-rate man of the world like this, so flat-looking with his ordinary, clean, rosy, uninteresting, self-satisfied, fundamentally bourgeois face. What a curse to have a dull son! A son like this, who could never understand his father. They had absolutely nothing, but nothing, in common, he and this neat, chubby, blue-eyed man. He was so pleased, thought Rogin, with all he owned and all he did and all he was that he could hardly unfasten his lip. Look at that lip, sticking up at the tip like a little thorn or egg tooth. He wouldn't give anyone the time of day. Would this perhaps be general forty years from now? Would personalities be chillier as the world aged and grew colder? The inhumanity of the next generation incensed Rogin. Father and son had no sign to make to each other. Terrible! Inhuman! What a vision of existence it gave him. Man's personal aims were nothing, illusion. The life force occupied each of us in turn in its progress toward its own fulfillment, trampling on our individual humanity, using us for its own ends like mere dinosaurs or bees, exploiting love heartlessly, making us engage in the social process, labor, struggle for money, and submit to the law of pressure, the universal law of layers, superimposition!

What the blazes am I getting into? Rogin thought. To be the father of a throwback to *her* father. The image of selfish blue eyes revolted Rogin. This was how his grandson would look. Joan, with whom Rogin was now more and more displeased, could not help that. For her, it was inevitable. But did it have to be inevitable for him? Well, then, Rogin, you fool, don't be a damned instrument. Get out of the way!

But it was too late for this, because he had already experienced the sensation of sitting next to his own son, his son and Joan's. He kept staring at him, waiting for him to say something, but the presumptive son remained coldly silent, though he must have been aware of Rogin's scrutiny. They even got out at the same stop — Sheridan Square. When they stepped to the platform, the man, without even looking at Rogin, went away in a different direction in his detestable blue checked coat, with his rosy, nasty face.

The whole thing upset Rogin very badly. When he approached Joan's door and heard Phyllis's little dog Henri barking even before he could knock, his face was very tense. I won't be used, he declared to himself. I have my own right to exist. Joan had better watch out. She had a light way of bypassing grave questions he had given earnest thought to. She always assumed no really disturbing thing would happen. He could not afford the luxury of such a carefree, debonair attitude himself, because he had to work hard and earn money so that disturbing things would *not* happen. Well, at the moment this situation could not be helped, and he really did not mind the money if he could feel that she was not necessarily the mother of such a son as his subway son or entirely the daughter of that awful, obscene father of hers. After all, Rogin was not himself so much like either of his parents, and quite different from his brother.

Joan came to the door, wearing one of Phyllis's expensive housecoats. It suited her very well. At first sight of her happy face, Rogin was brushed by the shadow of resemblance; the touch of it was extremely light, almost figmentary, but it made his flesh tremble.

She began to kiss him, saying, "Oh, my baby. You're covered with snow. Why didn't you wear your hat? It's all over its little head" — her favorite third-person endearment.

"Well, let me put down this bag of stuff. Let me take off my coat," grumbled Rogin, and escaped from her embrace. Why couldn't she wait making up to him? "It's so hot in here. My face is burning. Why do you keep the place at this temperature? And that damned dog keeps barking. If you didn't keep it cooped up, it wouldn't be so spoiled and noisy. Why doesn't anybody ever walk him?"

"Oh, it's not really so hot here! You've just come in from the cold. Don't you think this housecoat fits me better than Phyllis? Especially across the hips. She thinks so, too. She may sell it to me."

"I hope not," Rogin almost exclaimed.

She brought a towel to dry the melting snow from his short black hair. The flurry of rubbing excited Henri intolerably, and Joan locked him up in the bedroom where he jumped persistently against the door with a rhythmic sound of claws on the wood.

Joan said, "Did you bring the shampoo?"

"Here it is."

"Then, I'll wash your hair before dinner. Come."

"I don't want it washed."

"Oh, come on," she said, laughing.

Her lack of consciousness of guilt amazed him. He did not see how it could be. And the carpeted, furnished, lamplit, curtained room seemed to stand against his vision. So that he felt accusing and angry, his spirit sore and bitter, but it did not seem fitting to say why. Indeed, he began to worry lest the reason for it all slip away from him.

They took off his coat and his shirt in the bathroom, and she filled the sink. Rogin was full of his troubled emotions; now that his chest was bare, he could feel them even more and he said to himself, I'll have a thing or two to tell her pretty soon. I'm not letting them get away with it. "Do you think," he was going to tell her, "that I alone was made to carry the burden of the whole world on me? Do you think I was born to be taken advantage of and sacrificed? Do you think I'm just a natural resource, like a coal mine, or oil well, or fishery, or the like? Remember, that I'm a man is no reason why I should be loaded down. I have a soul in me no bigger or stronger than yours.

"Take away the externals, like the muscles, deeper voice, and so forth, and what remains? A pair of spirits, practically alike. So why shouldn't there also be equality? I can't always be the strong one."

"Sit here," said Joan, bringing up a kitchen stool to the sink. "Your hair's gotten all matted."

He sat with his breast against the cool enamel, his chin on the edge of the basin, the green, hot, radiant water reflecting the glass and the tile, and the sweet, cool, fragrant juice of the shampoo poured on his head. She began to wash him.

"You have the healthiest-looking scalp," she said. "It's all pink."

He answered, "Well, it should be white. There must be something wrong with me."

"But there's absolutely nothing wrong with you," she said, and pressed against him from behind, surrounding him, pouring the water gently over him until it seemed to him that the water came from within him, it was the warm fluid of his own secret loving spirit overflowing into the sink, green and foaming, and the words he had rehearsed he forgot, and his anger at his son-to-be disappeared altogether, and he sighed, and said to her from the water-filled hollow of the sink, "You always have such wonderful ideas, Joan. You know? You have a kind of instinct, a regular gift."

Biographical Notes

Saul Bellow, born in 1915 of Russian Jewish immigrant parents in Quebec, Canada, was brought up in Chicago and educated at the University of Chicago. Bellow, who has published nine novels to date and who has won the National Book Award three times, is considered by many critics to be the most accomplished of living American writers. Most of his fiction depicts outsiders and alienated men in search of love or some purpose in life which will end their isolation. In 1976 Bellow was awarded the Nobel Prize for Literature.

"A Father-to-Be", which first appeared in The New Yorker *in 1955, was later included in his collection of short stories* Mosby's Memoirs *(1968).*

Annotations

41 1 **Rogin** ['rɒdʒɪn] – 4 **dependable** reliable – **stocky** heavily built but not tall – 5 **Burberry** a light waterproof raincoat – **preposterous** absurd – 6 **gait** way of walking – 19 **divorcee** woman whose marriage is legally ended – 26 **to put s.o. through college** to finance s.o.'s college education – **annuity** fixed sum of money paid each year – 30 **to clerk** [ɑ:] *A.E.* [ɜ:] to work as a salesperson – **dime store** store where low-priced articles are sold

42 2 **osteopath** person who treats illnesses by moving and pressing muscles and bones – 4 **velvet** a thick soft cloth (Samt) – **frog fastener** a button and a loop which are used to do up a coat (Schlaufe) – **pouch** [aʊ] *here:* a small bag for tabacco – 5 **garnet** red, glasslike mineral used in jewellery – **brooch** [əʊ] large ornamental pin worn on a dress or coat – 6 **pewter** a mixture of metals including tin; something made from this – 13 **rug** carpet – 16 **superimposition** the placing of one thing on top of another – 22 **to choke s.o.** to stop s.o.'s breathing by blocking the supply of air – 23 **affliction** state of pain or suffering – 28 **cheer** state of hope, happiness – 29 **receding** *here:* showing larger areas of the teeth than are usually seen – **gum** area of flesh in which the teeth are set – **to kid** *coll.* to make fun of s.o. playfully – 33 **ferociously** *here:* greatly – 34 **pickle** vegetables kept in a special salt water mixture – 36 **chopped** *here:* cut into slices – 38 **soppy** thoroughly wet – **stale** no longer fresh – 40 **gaze** steady fixed look

43 4 **display** *here:* goods exhibited for customers – **chico** *Spanish for:* small boy – 5 **Pancho Villa** Mexican general and revolutionary leader (1877–1923) – 6 **to smear** to apply s.th. sticky or dirty to a surface – **to stake s.o. down/out** to tie s.o. down on the ground with wooden posts and ropes – 7 **toadlike** like a large ugly frog – **stout** strong, powerful – **to clasp** to hold tightly – 9 **Albany** capital of New York State – 10 **abuse** unjust practice – **realm** [e] sphere, region – 11 **clemency** mildness – 13 **braid** decorative edging for clothes – **chaps** protective coverings to prevent the legs from getting sore when riding – **spur** U-shaped piece of metal worn on the heel by horsemen – **gauntlet** ['gɔ:ntlɪt] long glove which covers the wrist – 14 **to unhook** to take off a hook – 15 **cookie** biscuit – 22 **gherkin** small green cucumber – 25 **endearment** a word or phrase expressing love – 26 **complexion** natural color or appearance of the face – 27 **defiant** [dɪ'faɪənt] not willing to accept authority or traditional ways of thinking – 29 **odorous** ['əʊdərəs] *here:* full of (unpleasant) smells – **captive** which cannot escape – 30 **to divert** to turn in another direction – **confession** admission that one has done s.th. wrong – 32 **suit of chain mail** protective clothing made of metal worn by knights in the Middle Ages

44 1 **austere** [ɔ:'stɪər] hard, simple – 3 **wattle** red flesh, growing from the head or throat of some birds – 7 **to soothe** to calm – 14 **to illuminate** *here:* to make clear with knowledge – 15 **to sway** to move first to one side and then to the other – 16 **bladder** bag in which urine collects in the body (Blase) – 18 **compound** ['--] substance made up of two or more parts combined – 19 **albumen** ['ælbjʊmən] white part of an egg – 29 **clairvoyant** [kleər'vɔɪənt] having a keen perception or great insight – 34 **snub-nosed** having a short and turned-up nose – 38 **aisle** [aɪl] passage between rows of seats – **knightly** *here:* brave or noble, of a knight

45 1 **vain of it** *here:* admiring it greatly – 2 **scowling** [aʊ] expressing a bad temper – 4 **car** *here:* one part of a train – 6 **contentious** tending to argue, ready to quarrel – 8 **foible** small personal weakness of which a person is wrongly proud – 13 **dwarf** person much smaller than the usual size – 16 **oxford** type of low shoe fastened over the instep – **seam** line where two edges of cloth or leather are joined – 18 **instep** part of shoe covering the surface of the foot between the toes and the ankle – 20 **dent** small hollows caused by blows or pressure – **puffy** rather swollen – 23 **Walter de la Mare** English poet and writer (1873–1956) – **midget** dwarf – **to take a resolve** to make a decision – 27 **fertile** full of ideas, plans, etc. – 28 **subtlety** ['sʌtəltɪ] cleverness in understanding or noticing – **rider** *here:* passenger – 31 **spice** substance used to make food taste better – 32 **sex determination** the fixing of the sex by the chromosomes – 33 **hereditary** [-'- - - -] passed down from parent to child – **linkage** connection – **uterus** organ in which a baby is carried before it is born – 34 **tax exemption** example of being freed from paying taxes – 35 **undertaker** person whose business is to manage funerals

46 3 **sturdy** strong – 6 **suède** [sweɪd] soft leather made from the skin of goats – 7 **cumbersome** heavy and difficult to carry – 8 **dandy** man who pays too much attention to his clothes – 9 **flaunting** showing off in order to attract attention – 21 **to detest** to hate strongly – 22 **hence** from now – 24 **trait** quality or characteristic – **heritage** ['herɪdɪdʒ] *here:* the characteristics passed on from parents to children – 26 **to hurtle** to speed or rush violently – 28 **transit** 1. transportation, 2. the shortness of life – 36 **to toil** to work long or hard at a task

47 2 **chubby** slightly fat – 5 **egg tooth** the hard tip on the beak of a baby bird which it uses to break through the eggshell – **He wouldn't give anyone the time of day.** He was not even willing to say hello to s.o. – 7 **chilly** without warmth of feeling – 8 **to incense** [-'-] to fill with anger – 12 **mere** not more than – 16 **What the blazes** *euphemism for:* What the hell – 17 **throwback** return to the typical qualities of one's forefathers – 24 **presumptive** *here:* imagined – 25 **scrutiny** close inspection – 28 **detestable** hateful, deserving to be hated – 36 **debonair** [ˌdebə'neə] cheerful, light-hearted

48 6 **figmentary** invented or imagined – 12 **wait making up to him** wait to make friends with him again – 14 **to coop up** to confine in a small space – 21 **flurry** short, sudden rush of activity – 23 **claw** [ɔː] the pointed nail on the foot of an animal – 33 **lest** (after expressions of fear, worry, anxiety, etc.) that

49 2 **to be loaded down** to be weighed down by a heavy burden – 4 **externals** *here:* the observable parts of a human being – 7 **sink** place in the kitchen used for washing dishes, vegetables, etc. – 8 **matted** twisted in a thick mass – 9 **enamel** [-'- -] glass-like substance used for protecting basins, baths, etc. (Emaille) – 10 **tile** covering for roofs, walls, etc. (Kachel) – 19 **fluid** substance which is able to flow, is capable of change – 20 **to rehearse** [rɪ'hɜːrs] to practise for later use

Bernard Malamud
The Mourners

Kessler, formerly an egg candler, lived alone on social security. Though past sixty-five, he might have found well-paying work with more than one butter and egg wholesaler, for he sorted and graded with speed and accuracy, but he was a quarrelsome type and considered a trouble maker, so the wholesalers did without him. Therefore, after a time he retired, living with few wants on his old-age pension. Kessler inhabited a small cheap flat on the top floor of a decrepit tenement on the East Side. Perhaps because he lived above so many stairs, no one bothered to visit him. He was much alone, as he had been most of his life. At one time he'd had a family, but unable to stand his wife or children, always in his way, he had after some years walked out on them. He never saw them thereafter, because he never sought them, and they did not seek him. Thirty years had passed. He had no idea where they were, nor did he think much about it.

In the tenement, although he had lived there ten years, he was more or less unknown. The tenants on both sides of his flat on the fifth floor, an Italian familiy of three middle-aged sons and their wizened mother, and a sullen, childless German couple named Hoffman, never said hello to him, nor did he greet any of them on the way up or down the narrow wooden stairs. Others of the house recognized Kessler when they passed him in the street, but they thought he lived elsewhere on the block. Ignace, the small, bent-back janitor, knew him best, for they had several times played two-handed pinochle; but Ignace, usually the loser because he lacked skill at cards, had stopped going up after a time. He complained to his wife that he couldn't stand the stink there, that the filthy flat with its junky furniture made him sick. The janitor had spread the word about Kessler to the others on the floor, and they shunned him as a dirty old man. Kessler understood this but had contempt for them all.

One day Ignace and Kessler began a quarrel over the way the egg candler piled oily bags overflowing with garbage into the dumb-waiter, instead of using a pail. One word shot off another, and they were soon calling each other savage names, when Kessler slammed the door in the janitor's face. Ignace ran down five flights of stairs and loudly cursed out the old man to his impassive wife. It happened that Gruber, the landlord, a fat man with a consistently worried face, who wore yards of baggy clothes, was in the building, making a check of plumbing repairs, and to him the enraged Ignace related the trouble he was having with Kessler. He described, holding his nose, the smell in Kessler's flat, and called him the dirtiest person he had ever seen. Gruber knew his janitor was exaggerating, but he felt burdened by financial worries which shot his blood pressure up to astonishing heights, so he settled it quickly by saying, "Give him notice." None of the tenants in the house had held a written lease since the war, and Gruber felt confident, in case somebody asked questions, that he could easily justify his dismissal of Kessler as an undesirable tenant. It had occurred to him that Ignace could then slap a cheap coat of paint on the walls and the flat would be let to someone for five dollars more than the old man was paying.

That night after supper, Ignace victoriously ascended the stairs and knocked on Kessler's door. The egg candler opened it, and seeing who stood there, immediately slammed it shut. Ignace shouted through the door, "Mr. Gruber says to give notice. We don't want you around here. Your dirt stinks the whole house." There was silence, but Ignace waited, relishing what he had said. Although after five minutes he still heard no sound, the janitor stayed there, picturing the old Jew trembling behind the locked door. He spoke again, "You got two weeks' notice till the first, then you better move out or Mr. Gruber and myself will throw you out." Ignace watched as the door slowly opened. To his surprise he found himself frightened at the old man's appearance. He looked, in the act of opening the door, like a corpse adjusting his coffin lid. But if he appeared dead, his voice was alive. It rose terrifyingly harsh from his throat, and he sprayed curses over all the years of Ignace's life. His eyes were reddened, his cheeks sunken, and his wisp of beard moved agitatedly. He seemed to be losing weight as he shouted. The janitor no longer had any heart for the matter, but he could not bear so many insults all at once so he cried out, "You dirty old bum, you better get out and don't make so much trouble." To this the enraged Kessler swore they would first have to kill him and drag him out dead.

On the morning of the first of December, Ignace found in his letter box a soiled folded paper containing Kessler's twenty-five dollars. He showed it to Gruber that evening when the landlord came to collect the rent money. Gruber, after a minute of absently contemplating the money, frowned disgustedly.

"I thought I told you to give notice."

"Yes, Mr. Gruber," Ignace agreed. "I gave him."

"That's a helluva chuzpah," said Gruber. "Gimme the keys."

Ignace brought the ring of pass keys, and Gruber, breathing heavily, began the lumbering climb up the long avenue of stairs. Although he rested on each landing, the fatigue of climbing, and his profuse flowing perspiration, heightened his irritation.

Arriving at the top floor he banged his fist on Kessler's door. "Gruber, the landlord. Open up here."

There was no answer, no movement within, so Gruber inserted the key into the lock and twisted. Kessler had barricaded the door with a chest and some chairs. Gruber had to put his shoulder to the door and shove before he could step into the hallway of the badly-lit two and a half room flat. The old man, his face drained of blood, was standing in the kitchen doorway.

"I warned you to scram outa here," Gruber said loudly. "Move out or I'll telephone the city marshal."

"Mr. Gruber —" began Kessler.

"Don't bother me with your lousy excuses, just beat it." He gazed around. "It looks like a junk shop and it smells like a toilet. It'll take me a month to clean up here."

"This smell is only cabbage that I am cooking for my supper. Wait, I'll open a window and it will go away."

"When you go away, it'll go away." Gruber took out his bulky wallet, counted out twelve dollars, added fifty cents, and plunked the money on top of the chest. "You got two more weeks till the fifteenth, then you gotta be out or I will get a dispossess. Don't talk back talk. Get outa here and go somewhere that they don't know you and maybe you'll get a place."

"No, Mr. Gruber," Kessler cried passionately. "I didn't do nothing, and I will stay here."

"Don't monkey with my blood pressure," said Gruber. "If you're not out by the fifteenth, I will personally throw you on your bony ass."

Then he left and walked heavily down the stairs.

The fifteenth came and Ignace found the twelve fifty in his letter box. He telephoned Gruber and told him.

"I'll get a dispossess," Gruber shouted. He instructed the janitor to write out a note saying to Kessler that his money was refused and to stick it under his door. This Ignace did. Kessler returned the money to the letter box, but again Ignace wrote a note and slipped it, with the money, under the old man's door.

After another day Kessler received a copy of his eviction notice. It said to appear in court on Friday at 10 A.M. to show cause why he should not be evicted for continued neglect and destruction of rental property. The official notice filled Kessler with great fright because he had never in his life been to court. He did not appear on the day he had been ordered to.

That same afternoon the marshal appeared with two brawny assistants. Ignace opened Kessler's lock for them and as they pushed their way into the flat, the janitor hastily ran down the stairs to hide in the cellar. Despite Kessler's wailing and carrying on, the two assistants methodically removed his meager furniture and set it out on the sidewalk. After that they got Kessler out, though they had to break open the bathroom door because the old man had locked himself in there. He shouted, struggled, pleaded with his neighbors to help him, but they looked on in a silent group outside the door. The two assistants, holding the old man tightly by the arms and skinny legs, carried him, kicking and moaning, down the stairs. They sat him in the street on a chair amid his junk. Upstairs, the marshal bolted the door with a lock Ignace had supplied, signed a paper which he handed to the janitor's wife, and then drove off in an automobile with his assistants.

Kessler sat on a split chair on the sidewalk. It was raining and the rain soon turned to sleet, but he still sat there. People passing by skirted the pile of his belongings. They stared at Kessler and he stared at nothing. He wore no hat or coat, and the snow fell on him, making him look like a piece of his dispossessed goods. Soon the wizened Italian woman from the top floor returned to the house with two of her sons, each carrying a loaded shopping bag. When she recognized Kessler sitting amid his furniture, she began to shriek. She shrieked in Italian at Kessler although he paid no attention to her. She stood on the stoop, shrunken, gesticulating with thin arms, her loose mouth working angrily. Her sons tried to calm her, but still she shrieked. Several of the neighbors came down to see who was making the racket. Finally, the two sons, unable to think what else to do, set down their shopping bags, lifted Kessler out of the chair, and carried him up the stairs. Hoffman, Kessler's other neighbor, working with a small triangular file, cut open the padlock, and Kessler was carried into the flat from which he had been evicted. Ignace screeched at everybody, calling them filthy names, but the three men went downstairs and hauled up Kessler's chairs, his broken table, chest, and ancient metal bed. They piled all the furniture into the bedroom. Kessler sat on the edge of the bed and wept. After a while, after the old Italian woman had sent in a soup plate full of hot macaroni seasoned with tomato sauce and grated cheese, they left.

Ignace phoned Gruber. The landlord was eating and the food turned to lumps in his throat. "I'll throw them all out, the bastards," he yelled. He put on his hat, got into his car and drove through the slush to the tenement. All the time he was thinking of his worries: high repair costs; it was hard to keep the place together; maybe the building would someday collapse. He had read of such things. All of a sudden the front of the building parted from the rest and fell like a breaking wave into the street. Gruber cursed the old man for taking him from his supper. When he got to the house he snatched Ignace's keys and ascended the sagging stairs. Ignace tried to follow, but Gruber told him to stay the hell in his hole. When the landlord was not looking, Ignace crept up after him.

Gruber turned the key and let himself into Kessler's dark flat. He pulled the light chain and found the old man sitting limply on the side of the bed. On the floor at his feet lay a plate of stiffened macaroni.

"What do you think you're doing here?" Gruber thundered.

The old man sat motionless.

"Don't you know it's against the law? This is trespassing and you're breaking the law. Answer me."

Kessler remained mute.

Gruber mopped his brow with a large yellowed handkerchief.

"Listen, my friend, you're gonna make lots of trouble for yourself. If they catch you in here you might go to the workhouse. I'm only trying to advise you."

To his surprise Kessler looked at him with wet, brimming eyes.

"What did I did to you?" he bitterly wept. "Who throws out of his house a man that he lived there ten years and pays every month on time his rent? What did I do, tell me? Who hurts a man without a reason? Are you a Hitler or a Jew?" He was hitting his chest with his fist.

Gruber removed his hat. He listened carefully, at first at a loss what to say, but then answered: "Listen, Kessler, it's not personal. I own this house and it's falling apart. My bills are sky high. If the tenants don't take care they have to go. You don't take care and you fight with my janitor, so you have to go. Leave in the morning, and I won't say another word. But if you don't leave the flat, you'll get the heave-ho again. I'll call the marshal."

"Mr. Gruber," said Kessler, "I won't go. Kill me if you want it, but I won't go."

Ignace hurried away from the door as Gruber left in anger. The next morning, after a restless night of worries, the landlord set out to drive to the city marshal's office. On the way he stopped at a candy store for a pack of cigarettes, and there decided once more to speak to Kessler. A thought had occurred to him: he would offer to get the old man into a public home.

He drove to the tenement and knocked on Ignace's door.

"Is the old gink still up there?"

"I don't know if so, Mr. Gruber." The janitor was ill at ease.

"What do you mean you don't know?"
"I didn't see him go out. Before, I looked in his keyhole but nothing moves."
"So why didn't you open the door with your key?"
"I was afraid," Ignace answered nervously.
"What are you afraid?"
Ignace wouldn't say.
A fright went through Gruber but he didn't show it. He grabbed the keys and walked ponderously up the stairs, hurrying every so often. No one answered his knock. As he unlocked the door he broke into heavy sweat.

But the old man was there, alive, sitting without shoes on the bedroom floor.

"Listen, Kessler," said the landlord, relieved although his head pounded. "I got an idea that, if you do it the way I say, your troubles are over."

He explained his proposal to Kessler, but the egg candler was not listening. His eyes were downcast, and his body swayed slowly sideways. As the landlord talked on, the old man was thinking of what had whirled through his mind as he had sat out on the sidewalk in the falling snow. He had thought through his miserable life, remembering how, as a young man, he had abandoned his family, walking out on his wife and three innocent children, without even in some way attempting to provide for them; without, in all the intervening years — so God help him — once trying to discover if they were alive or dead. How, in so short a life, could a man do so much wrong? This thought smote him to the heart and he recalled the past without end and moaned and tore at his flesh with his fingernails.

Gruber was frightened at the extent of Kessler's suffering. Maybe I should let him stay, he thought. Then as he watched the old man, he realized he was bunched up there on the floor engaged in an act of mourning. There he sat, white from fasting, rocking back and forth, his beard dwindled to a shade of itself.

Something's wrong here — Gruber tried to imagine what and found it all oppressive. He felt he ought to run out, get away, but then saw himself fall and go tumbling down the five flights of stairs; he groaned at the broken picture of himself lying at the bottom. Only he was still there in Kessler's bedroom, listening to the old man praying. Somebody's dead, Gruber muttered. He figured Kessler had got bad news, yet instinctively knew he hadn't. Then it struck him with a terrible force that the mourner was mourning him: it was *he* who was dead.

The landlord was agonized. Sweating brutally, he felt an enormous constricted weight in him that slowly forced itself up, until his head was at the point of bursting. For a full minute he awaited a stroke; but the feeling painfully passed, leaving him miserable.

When after a while, he gazed around the room, it was clean, drenched in
5 daylight and fragrance. Gruber then suffered unbearable remorse for the way he had treated the old man.

At last he could stand it no longer. With a cry of shame he tore the sheet off Kessler's bed, and wrapping it around his bulk, sank heavily to the floor and became a mourner.

Biographical Notes

Bernard Malamud was born in 1914 of Russian Jewish immigrant parents and grew up in New York City. In 1942 he graduated from Columbia University, New York City, and later taught English literature at Oregon State University, then at Bennington College, Vermont. In addition to his numerous short fictional writings, he is the author of such well-known novels as The Assistant *(1957),* The Tenants *(1971) and* Dubin's Lives *(1979). In his fiction, which often portrays a typical Jewish American environment, Malamud is preoccupied with the unhappy experiences of Jews and in particular with the experience of suffering, which he sees as a way towards man's enlightenment.*

"The Mourners" first appeared in Discovery *in 1955 and was later included in his collection of stories* The Magic Barrel *(1958), which won him the National Book Award in 1959.*

Annotations

52 **mourner** [ɔː] person who shows sorrow for a dead person – 1 **egg candler** person who examines eggs by holding them in front of light – 3 **wholesaler** businessman who sells goods to shopkeepers – **to grade** to classify according to quality – 7 **decrepit** in a very bad state of repair – **tenement** a house with rented apartments, esp. one in the poorer parts of a city – **(Lower) East Side** south-east part of Manhattan where many Jewish immigrants used to live – 11 **to walk out on s.o.** to leave s.o. suddenly – 16 **wizened** [ɪ] reduced in size by age – 21 **janitor** person who is employed to look after a building – 22 **pinochle** ['piːnɒkl] a game played with 48 cards – 24 **junky** worthless – 26 **to shun** to

avoid – 27 **contempt** [-'-] attitude of considering other people worthless – 29 **dumb-waiter** small elevator used for sending food or rubbish between floors – 30 **pail** bucket, container – 32 **to curse out** to swear about

53 1 **impassive** indifferent, showing no signs of feeling – 3 **plumbing** ['plʌmɪŋ] the water-pipes and water-tanks in a building – 8 **to give s.o. notice** *here:* to tell s.o. to leave his flat at the end of the month – 9 **tenant** person who rents a flat in a tenement house – **lease** [s] contract (of rent) – 11 **dismissal** removal, sending away – 19 **to relish** to enjoy greatly – 25 **coffin** box in which a dead person is laid for burial – **lid** piece covering the top of a box or container – 28 **wisp** *here:* small bundle of hair – 31 **bum** *sl.* beggar, tramp – 35 **soiled** dirty – 3 **to frown** to draw the eyebrows together (in order to express displeasure)

54 1 **helluva** ['---] *sl.* hell of a – **chuzpah** ['xʊtspə] *Yiddish:* bold rudeness and arrogance – 2 **pass key** key which opens all the doors in a house – 3 **lumbering** *here:* difficult – 4 **profuse** free, plentiful – 8 **to insert** to put in – 12 **to drain** *here:* become empty – 13 **to scram** *coll.* to get out, to go away quickly – 16 **to beat it** *coll.* to go away, to get out – 17 **junk shop** a shop which sells old things which are often worthless – 21 **bulky** large and heavy – 22 **to plunk** to put down heavily or suddenly – 24 **dispossess** official order to leave a flat or house – **back talk** rude talk in reply to s.o. – 28 **to monkey with** *coll.* to play around with – 29 **ass** *sl.* behind – 38 **eviction notice** court order instructing a tenant to leave – 39 **to show cause** to state reasons

55 3 **brawny** strong, muscular – 6 **wailing** loud cries expressing grief – **carrying on** *coll.* behaving in an excited, silly way – 7 **meager** (*B.E.:* meagre) poor, insufficient – 9 **to plead** to ask earnestly – 12 **to moan** to make sounds expressing suffering – 13 **to bolt** *here:* to lock – 16 **split** broken into two or more parts – 17 **sleet** partly frozen rain – **to skirt** to go around – 23 **to shriek** [i:] to scream shrilly – 24 **stoop** small porch at the entrance of a house – 27 **racket** loud noise – 29 **file** steel tool used for cutting or smoothing hard surfaces – 30 **padlock** removable lock – 31 **to screech** to scream in anger or pain – 32 **to haul up** [hɔ:l] to pull with effort or force – 35 **seasoned with sauce** with sauce to make it taste better – **to grate** to rub into small pieces – 39 **slush** partly melted snow

56 5 **to sag** to sink or hang down in the middle under weight or pressure – 9 **limply** not stiff or firm, having lost all energy – 13 **to trespass** ['---] to go on privately owned land or property without permission – 15 **mute** silent, making no sound – 16 **to mop** to wipe s.th. – **brow** [aʊ] forehead – 18 **workhouse** *here:* kind of prison where offenders are made to work – 20 **brimming** *here:* full of tears – 30 **to get the heave-ho** *coll.* to get thrown out – 39 **gink** *sl.* unpleasant man

57 9 **ponderously** heavily, with great effort – 14 **his head pounded** he felt heavy, regular blows inside his head – 17 **to sway** to move first to one side and then to the other – 25 **to smite (smote, smitten)** to strike – 29 **to be bunched up** to sit with one's legs and arms held close to one's body – **mourning** expression of grief and suffering over s.o.'s death – 30 **to fast** to go without food, esp. as a religious duty – 31 **to dwindle** to become less or smaller – 40 **to be agonized** to be in great pain

58 4 **to be drenched in** to be bathed in or filled completely with – 5 **remorse** deep sense of guilt and regret – 8 **bulk** *here:* large body

Joyce Carol Oates

Out of Place

I have this memory: I am waiting in line for a movie. The line is long, noisy, restless, mostly kids my age (I seem to be about thirteen). The movie must be ... a Western, I think. I can almost see the posters and I think I see a man with a cowboy hat. Good. I do see this man and I see a horse on the poster, it is all becoming clear. A Western. I am a kid, thirteen, but not like the thirteen-year-olds who pass by the hospital here on their way home from school — they are older than I was at that age, everyone seems older. I am nineteen now, I think. I will be twenty in a few weeks and my mother talks about how I will be home, then, in time for my birthday. That gives her pleasure and so I like to hear her talk about it. But my memory is more important: the movie house, yes, and the kids, and I am one of them. We are all jostling together, moving foreward in surges, a bunch of us from St. Ann's Junior High. Other kids are there from Clinton, which is a tough school. We are all in line waiting and no one is out of line. I am there, with them. We shuffle up to the ticket window and buy our tickets (50¢) and go inside, running.

There is something pleasant about this memory, but dwelling upon memories is unhealthy. They tell me that. They are afraid I will remember the explosion, and my friend who died, but I have already forgotten these things. There is no secret about it, of course. Everything is open. We were caught in a land mine explosion and some of us were luckier than others, we weren't killed, that's all. I am very lucky to be alive. I am not being sarcastic but quite truthful, because in the end it is only truth you can stand. In camp, and for a while when we fooled around for so long without ever seeing the enemy, then some of the guys were sarcastic — but that went away. Everything falls away except truth and that is what you hang on to.

The truth is that my right leg is gone and that I have some trouble with my "vision." My eyes.

On sunny days we are wheeled outside, so that we can watch the school children playing across the street. The hospital is very clean and white, and there is a kind of patio or terrace or wide walk around the front and sides, where we can sit. Next door, some distance away, is a school that is evidently a grade school. The children play at certain times — ten-fifteen in the morning, at noon, and two in the afternoon. I don't know if they are always the same children. I have trouble with my "vision," it isn't the way it used to be and yet in a way I can't remember what it used to be like. My glasses are heavy and make red marks on my nose, and sometimes my skin is sore around my ears, but that is the only sign that the glasses are new. In a way nothing is new but has always been with me. That is why I am pleased with certain memories, like the memory of the Western movie. Though I do not remember the movie itself, but only waiting in line to get in the theater.

There is a boy named Ed here, a friend of mine. He was hurt at about the same time I was, though in another place. He is about twenty too. His eyes are as good as ever and he can see things I can't; I sometimes ask him to tell me about the playground and the children there. The playground is surrounded by a high wire fence and the children play inside this fence, on their swings and slides and teeter-totters, making a lot of noise. Their voices are very high and shrill. We don't mind the noise, we like it, but sometimes it reminds me of something — I can almost catch the memory but not quite. Cries and screams by themselves are not bad. I mean the sounds are not bad. But if you open your eyes wide you may have latched onto the wrong memory and might see the wrong things — screams that are not happy screams, etc. There was a boy somewhere who was holding on to the hand of his "buddy." ("Buddy" is a word I would not have used before, I don't know where I got it from exactly.) That boy was crying, because the other boy was dead — but I can't quite remember who they were. The memory comes and goes silently. It is nothing to be upset about. The doctor told us all that it is healthier to think about our problems, not to push them back. He is a neat, clean man dressed in white, a very kind man. Sometimes his face looks creased, there are too many wrinkles in it, and he looks like my father — they are about the same age.

I like the way my father calls him *Dr. Pritchard*. You can tell a man's worth by the way my father speaks to him, I know that sounds egotistical but it's true, and my father trusts Dr. Pritchard. It is different when he speaks to someone he doesn't quite trust, oh, for example, certain priests who look too young, too boyish; he hesitates before he calls them *Father*. He hesitates before he says hello to Father Presson, who comes here to see me and hear my confession and all, and then the words "Father Presson" come out a little forced.

"Look at that big kid, by the slide. See?" Ed says nervously.

I think I see him — a short blur of no-color by the slide. "What is he doing?"

"I don't know. I thought he was. . . . No, I don't know," Ed says.

There is a hesitation in Ed's voice too. Sometimes he seems not to know what he is saying, whether he should say it. I can hear the distance in his voice, the distance between the school children over there and us up here on the ledge, in the sun. When the children fight we feel nervous and we don't know what to do. Not that they really fight, not exactly. But sometimes the mood of the playground breaks and a new mood comes upon it. It's hard to explain it. Ed keeps watching for that though he doesn't want to see it.

Ed has a short, muscular body, and skin that always looks tanned. His hair is black, shaved off close, and his eyebrows of course are black and very thick. He looks hunched up in the wheel chair, about to spring off and run away. His legs just lie there, though, and never move. They are both uninjured. His problem is somewhere else, in his spine — it is a mysterious thing, how a bullet strikes in one place and damages another. We have all learned a lot about the body, here. I think I would like to be a doctor. I think that, to be a doctor like Dr. Pritchard, you must have a great reverence for the body and its springs and wires and tubes, I mean, you must understand how they work together, all together. It is a strange thing. When I tried to talk to my parents about this they acted strange. I told them that Ed and I both would like to be doctors, if things got better.

"Yes," my father said slowly, "the study of medicine is — is —"

"Very beneficial," my mother said.

"Yes, beneficial —"

Then they were silent. I said, "I mean if things get better. I know I couldn't get through medical school, the way I am now."

"I wouldn't be too sure of that," my father said. "You know how they keep discovering all these extraordinary things —"

(My father latches onto special words occasionally. Now it is the word "extraordinary." I don't know where he got it from, from a friend probably. He is a vice-president for a company that makes a certain kind of waxed paper and waxed cardboard.)

"But you will get better," my mother said. "You know that."

I am seized with a feeling of happiness. Not because of what my mother said, maybe it's true and maybe not, I don't know, but because of — the fact of doctors, the fact of the body itself which is such a mystery. I can't explain it. I said, groping for my words, "If this hadn't happened then — then — I guess I'd be just the way I was, I mean, I wouldn't know — what it's like to be like this." But that was a stupid thing to say. Mother began crying again, it was embarrassing. With my glasses off, lying back against the pillow, I could pretend that I didn't notice; so I said, speaking in my new voice which is a little too slow and stumbling, "I mean — there are lots of things that are mysteries — like the way the spine hooks up with things — and the brain — and — and by myself I wouldn't know about these things —"

But it's better to talk about other matters. In my room, away from the other patients, the talk brought to me by my parents and relatives and friends is like a gift from the outside, and it has the quality of the spring days that are here now: sunny and fragrant but very delicate. My visitors' words are like rays of sunlight. It might seem that you could grab hold of them and sit up, but you can't, they're nothing, they don't last — they are gifts, that's all, like the other gifts I have. For instance, my mother says: "Betty is back now. She wants to know when she can see you, but I thought that could wait."

"Oh, is she back?"

"She didn't have a very happy time, you know."

"What's she doing now?"

"Oh, nothing, I don't know. She might go to school."

"Where?"

"A community college, nothing much."

"That's nice."

This conversation is about a cousin of mine who married some jerk and ran away to live in Mexico. But the conversation is not really about her. I don't know what it is about. It is "about" the words themselves. When my mother says, "Betty is back now," that means "Betty-is-back-now" is being talked about, not the girl herself. We hardly know the girl herself. Then we move on to talk about Harold Spender, who is a bachelor friend of my father's. Harold Spender has a funny name and Mother likes him for his name. He is always "spending" too much money. I think he has expensive parties or something, I don't know. But "Harold Spender" is another gift, and I think this gift means: "You see, everything is still the same, your cousin is still a dope and Harold Spender is still with us, spending money. Nothing has changed."

Sometimes when they are here, visiting, and Mother chatters on like that, a terrible door opens in my mind and I can't hear her. It is like waking up at night when you don't know it is night. A door opens and though I know Mother is still talking, I can't hear her. This lasts a few seconds, no more. I go into it and come out of it and no one notices. The door opens by itself, silently, and beyond it everything is black and very quiet, just nothing.

But sometimes I am nervous and feel very sharp. That is a peculiar word, sharp. I mean my body tenses and I seem to be sitting forward and my hands grip the arms of the chair, as if I'm about to throw myself out of it and demand something. Demand something! Ed's voice gets like that too. It gets very thin and demanding and sometimes he begins to cry. It's better to turn away from that, from a boy of twenty crying. I don't know why I get nervous. There is no relationship between what my body feels and what is going on outside, and that is what frightens me.

Dr. Pritchard says there is nothing to be frightened about any longer. Nothing.

He is right, of course. I think it will be nice when I am home again and the regular routine begins. My nervousness will go away and there will not be the strange threat of that door, which opens so silently and invites me in. And Father won't take so much time off from work, and Mother will not chatter so. It will be nice to get back into place and decide what I will do, though there is no hurry about that. When I was in high school I fooled around too much. It wasn't because of basketball either, that was just an excuse, I wasted time and so did the other kids. I wore trousers the color of bone that were pretty short and tight, and I fooled around with my hair, nothing greasy but pretty long in front, flipped down onto my forehead. Mr. Palisano, the physics teacher, was also the basketball coach and he always said: "Hey, Furlong, what's your hurry? Just what's your hurry?" He had a teasing singsong voice he used only on kids he liked. He was a tall, skinny man, a very intelligent man. "Just what's your hurry?" he said when I handed in my physics problems half-finished, or made a fool of myself in basketball practice. He was happy when I told him I was going into physics, but when I failed the first course I didn't want to go back and tell him — the hell with it. So I switched into math because I had to take math anyway. And then what happened? I don't remember. I was just a kid then, I fooled around too much. The kids at the school — it was a middle-sized school run by Holy Cross fathers, who also run Notre Dame — just fooled around too much, some of them flunked out. I don't think I flunked out. It gives me a headache to think about it —

To think about the kids in my calculus class, that gives me a headache. I don't know why. I can remember my notebook, and the rows of desks, and the blackboard (though it was green), and the bell striking the hour from outside (though it was always a little off), and I think of it all like a bubble with the people still inside. All the kids and me among them, still in the same room, still there. I like to think of that.

But they aren't still there in that room. Everything has moved on. They have moved on to other rooms and I am out here, at this particular hospital. I wonder if I will be able to catch up with them. If I can read, if my eyes get better, I don't see why not. Father talks about me returning. It's no problem with a wheel chair these days, he says, and there is the business about the artificial "limb," etc. I think it will be nice to get back to books and reading and regular assignments.

I am thinking about high school, about the halls and the stairways. Mr. Palisano, and physics class, and the afternoon basketball games. I am thinking about the excitement of those games, which was not quite fear, and about the drive back home, in my car or someone else's. I went out a lot. And one night, coming home from a dance, I saw a car parked and a man fooling around by it so I stopped to help him. "Jesus Christ," he kept saying. He had a flat tire and he was very angry. He kept snuffling and wiping his nose on his shoulder, very angry, saying "Jesus Christ" and other things, other words, not the way the kids said them but in a different way — hard to explain. It made me understand that adults had made up those words, not in play but out of hatred. He was not kidding. The way he said those words frightened me. Fear comes up from the earth, the coldness of the earth, flowing up from your feet up your legs and into your bowels, like the clay of the earth itself, and your heart begins to hammer. . . .

I never told anyone about that night, what a fool I was to stop. What if something had happened to me?

I was ashamed of being such a fool. I always did stupid things, always went out of my way and turned out looking like a fool. Then I'd feel shame and not tell anyone. For instance, I am ashamed about something that happened here in the hospital a few days ago. I think it will be nice when I am home again, back in my room, where these things can't happen. There was myself and Ed and another man, out on the terrace by the side entrance, in the sun, and these kids came along. It was funny because they caught my eye when they drove past in a convertible, and they must have turned into the parking lot and got out. They were visiting someone in the hospital. The girl was carrying a grocery bag that probably had fruit in it or something. She had long dark hair and bangs that fell down to her eyebrows, and she wore sunglasses, and bright blue stretch pants of the kind that have stirrups for the feet to keep them stretched down tight. The boy wore sunglasses too, slacks and a sweater, and sandals without socks. He had the critical, unsurprised look of kids from the big university downtown.

They came up the steps, talking. The girl swung her hair back like a horse, a pony — I mean, the motion reminded me of something like that. She looked over at us and stopped talking, and the boy looked too. They were my age. The girl hesitated but the boy kept on walking fast. He frowned. He seemed embarrassed. The girl came toward me, not quite walking directly toward me, and her mouth moved in an awkward smile. She said, "I know you, don't I? Don't I know you?"

I was very excited. I tried to tell her that with her sunglasses on I couldn't see her well. But when I tried to talk the words came out jumbled. She licked her lips nervously. She said, "Were you in the war? Vietnam?"

I nodded.

She stared at me. It was strange that her face showed nothing, unlike the other faces that are turned toward me all the time. The boy, already at the door, said in an irritated sharp voice: "Come on, we're late." The girl took a vague step backward, the way girls swing slowly away from people — you must have seen them often on sidewalks before ice cream parlors or schools? They stare as if fascinated at one person, while beginning the slow inevitable swing toward another who stands behind them. The boy said, opening the door: "Come on! He deserves it!"

They went inside. And then the shame began, an awful shame. I did not understand this though I thought about it a great deal. Someone came out to help me, a nurse. When I cry most people look away in embarrassment but the nurses show nothing, nothing at all. They boss me around a little. Crying makes me think of someone else crying, a soldier holding another soldier's hand, sitting in some rubble. One soldier is alive and the other dead, the one who is alive is holding the other's hand and crying, like a baby. Like a puppy. A kitten, a baby, something small and helpless, when the crying does no good and is not meant for any good.

I think that my name is Jack Furlong. There was another person named Private Furlong, evidently myself. Now I am back home and I am Jack Furlong again. I can imagine many parts of this city without really seeing them, and what is surprising — and very pleasant — is the way these memories come to me, so unexpected. Lying in bed with no thoughts at all I suddenly find myself thinking of a certain dime store where we hung out, by the comic book racks, many years ago; or I think of a certain playground on the edge of a ravine made by a glacier, many thousands of years ago. I don't know what makes these memories come to me but they exert a kind of tug — on my heart, I suppose. It's very strange. My eyes sometimes fill with tears, but a different kind of tears. I was never good at understanding feelings but now, in the hospital, I have a lot of time for thinking. I think that I am a kind of masterpiece. I mean, a miracle. My body and my brain. It is like a little world inside, or a factory, with everything functioning and the dynamo at the very center — my heart — pumping and pumping with no source of energy behind it. I think about that a lot. What keeps it going? And the eyes. Did you know that the eye is strong, very strong? That the muscles are like steel? Yes. Eyes are very strong, I mean the substance of the eyes is strong. It takes a lot to destroy them.

At last they check me out and bring me home — a happy day. It is good to be back home where everything is peaceful and familiar. When I lived in this house before I did not think about "living" in it, or about the house at all. Now, looking out of my window, I can see the front lawn and the street and the other houses facing us, all ranch houses, and I am aware of being very fortunate. A few kids are outside, racing past on bicycles. It is a spring day, very warm. The houses on the block make a kind of design if you look right. I am tired from all the exertion involved getting me here, and so it is difficult to explain what I mean — a design, a setting. Everything in place. It has not changed and won't change. It is a very pleasant neighborhood, and I think I remember hearing Mother once say that our house had cost $45,000. I had "heard" this remark years ago but never paid any attention to it. Now I keep thinking about it, I don't know why. There is something wonderful about that figure: it means something. Is it secret? It is the very opposite of rubble, yes. There are no screams here, no sudden explosions. Yes, I think that is why it pleases me so. I fall asleep thinking of forty-five thousand dollars.

My birthday. It is a few days later. I have been looking through the books in my room, a history textbook, a calculus textbook, and something called *College Rhetoric*. Those were my books and I can recognize my handwriting in the margins, but I have a hard time reading them now. To get away from the reading I look around — or the door in my mind begins to open slowly, scaring me, and so I wheel myself over to the window to look out. Father has just flown back from Boston. Yes, it is my birthday and I am twenty. We have a wheelchair of our own now, not the hospital's chair but our own. There is a wooden ramp from our side door right into the garage, and when they push me out I have a sudden sensation of panic right in my heart — do they know how to handle me? what if they push me too hard? They are sometimes clumsy and a little rough, accidentally. Whenever Father does something wrong I think at once, not meaning to, *They wouldn't do that at the hospital.*

My uncle and my aunt are coming too. We are going out to Skyway for dinner. This is a big restaurant and motel near the airport. There is the usual trouble getting me in and out of the car, but Father is getting used to it. My uncle Floyd keeps saying, "Well, it's great to have you back. I mean it. It's just great, it's just wonderful to have you back." My aunt is wearing a hat with big droopy yellow flowers on it, a pretty hat. But something about the flowers makes me think of giant leaves in the jungle, coated with dust and sweat, and the way the air tasted — it made your throat and lungs ache, the dust in the air. Grit. Things were flying in the air. Someone was screaming, "Don't leave me!" A lot of them were screaming that. But my father said, "We'd better hurry, our reservations are for six."

Six is early to eat, I know. They are hurrying up the evening because I get tired so fast. My uncle opens the door and my father wheels me inside, all of it done easily. My father says to a man, "Furlong, for five —" This restaurant is familiar. On one side there is a stairway going down, carpeted in blue, and down there are rooms for — oh, banquets and meetings and things. Ahead of us is a cocktail lounge, very dark. Off to the left, down a corridor lined with paintings (they are by local artists, for sale) is the restaurant we are going to, the Grotto Room. But the man is looking through his ledger. My mother says to my aunt, "I bought that watercolor here, you know, the one over the piano." The women talk about something but my uncle stares at my father and the manager, silent. Something is wrong. The manager looks through his book and his face is red and troubled. Finally he looks up and says, "Yes, all right. Down this way." He leads us down to the Grotto Room.

We are seated. The table is covered with a white tablecloth, a glaring white. A waitress is already at Father's elbow. She looks at us, her eyes darting around the table and lingering no longer on me than on anyone else. I know that my glasses are thick and that my face is not pleasant to look at, not the same face as before. But still she does not look at me more than a second maybe two seconds. Father orders drinks. It is my birthday. He glances over to the side and I see that someone at the next table, some men and women are watching us. A woman in red — I think it is red — does something with her napkin, putting it on the table. Father picks up his menu, which is very large. My mother and aunt chatter about something, my mother hands me a menu. At the next table a man stands. He changes places with the woman, and now her back is to our table. I understand this but pretend to notice nothing, look down at the menu with a pleased, surprised expression, because it is better this way. It is better for everyone.

"What do you think you'll order? Everything looks so tempting," she says.

They were in a hurry and the wounded and the dead were stacked together, brought back together in a truck. But not carried at the end of a nylon cord, from a helicopter, not that. This memory comes to me in a flash, then fades. I was driving the truck, I think. Wasn't I? I was on the truck. I did not hover at the end of a line, in a plastic sack. Those were others — I didn't know them, only saw them from a distance. They screamed: "Don't leave me!"

"Lobster," Father says. He speaks with certainty: he is predicting my choice for dinner. "I bet it's lobster, eh?"

"Lobster."

My mother squeezes my arm, pleased that I have given the right answer.

5 "My choice too," she says. "Always have fish on Fridays ... the old customs ... I like the old customs, no matter what people say. The Mass in Latin, and ... and priests who know what their vocations are. ... How do you want your lobster, dear? Broiled?"

"Yes."

10 "Or this way — here — the Skyway Lobster?" She leans over to help me with the menu, pointing at the words. There is a film, a gauzy panel between me and the words, and I keep waiting for it to disappear. The faces around the table, the voices ... the smiling mouths and eyes ... I keep glancing up at them, waiting for the veil to be yanked away. *He deserves it.*
15 *Don't leave me!* In the meantime I think I will have the Skyway Lobster.

"You're sure?"

"Yes."

"My own choice also," my mother says. She looks around the table, in triumph, and the faces smile back at her and at me.

Biographical Notes

Joyce Carol Oates (born 1938) grew up in New York State and is at present Professor of English at the University of Windsor in Ontario, Canada. Since the early 1960s she has published numerous collections of short stories as well as several novels, books of poetry and plays. From the start of her writing career she has earned many prestigious literary awards, among them the National Book Award in 1970 for her novel Them *and the O. Henry Award, a well-known American prize for short story writers. In many of her stories Ms. Oates depicts people in a state of psychological crisis who are suffering from a feeling of loss and despair.*

"Out of Place" first appeared in The Virginia Quarterly Review *in 1968 and was later included in* The Seduction and Other Stories.

Annotations

60   1 **in line** in a queue – 2 **to jostle** to push roughly (against one another) – **to move in surges** to go as in waves – 15 **to shuffle** to walk without lifting the feet – 17 **to dwell upon s.th.** to think about s.th. at length – 26 **to hang on to** to keep to, to hold onto tightly – 31 **patio** ['pætɪəʊ] paved area near a house used for outdoor living, terrace – **walk** path – 32 **evidently** obviously, apparently

61   1 **grade school** elementary school – 15 **swing** seat on which one can swing backwards and forwards – **slide** smooth slope for children to slip down on their behinds – **teeter-totter** long board on which children can rise and fall alternatively (Wippe) – 19 **to latch onto** *here:* to recall or select – 22 **buddy** *coll.* friend or comrade – 28 **creased** with lines in the skin – 39 **blur** indistinct outline or movement

62   5 **ledge** narrow flat surface coming out from a wall – 11 **to hunch up** to pull one's body into a rounded shape – 13 **spine** backbone – 17 **spring** *here:* muscle or part of the body which is elastic – 28 **to latch onto** *here:* to pick out and concentrate on – 33 **to seize** [i:] to take hold of suddenly and violently – 36 **to grope for** to search for as in the dark

63   2 **to hook up with** to connect with – 7 **fragrant** [eɪ] sweet-smelling – 8 **to grab hold of** to take hold of suddenly and roughly – 18 **community college** an institution offering courses on a college level to the residents of a town – 20 **jerk** *sl.* stupid person – 30 **dope** *sl.* stupid person – 39 **to tense** to become stiff

64   18 **coach** trainer – 20 **to tease** to make fun of playfully – 28 **(Congregation of) Holy Cross** a Roman Catholic order – **Notre Dame** Catholic University in Notre Dame, Indiana, run by the Holy Cross – 29 **to flunk out** *coll.* to fail in an exam; to give up one's college studies – 31 **calculus class** course of higher mathematics, such as differential calculus – 34 **bubble** a round body of gas in a thin envelope

65   2 **artificial limb** [lɪm] leg or arm made for someone who has had an amputation – 3 **assignment** task given to a student, often as homework – 10 **tire** *B.E.:* tyre – 15 **to kid** *coll.* to joke, to make fun – 17 **bowels** [aʊ] the food canals in the body below the stomach (Eingeweide) – **clay** stiff, sticky earth – 28 **convertible** car with a roof that can be folded back – 31 **bangs** hair worn over the forehead – 33 **stirrup** *here:* a loop of cloth through which the foot is put

66   4 **jumbled** confused, mixed up – 11 **ice cream parlor** store where young people meet and have ice cream – 20 **rubble** mass of broken stones – 25 **private** soldier of the lowest rank – 29 **dime store** shop which sells cheap articles – **to hang out** *coll.* to spend much of one's free time – 30 **rack** shelf, usually made of metal – 31 **ravine** [rə'viːn] deep narrow valley with steep sides – **glacier** ['glæsɪə *A.E.:* 'gleɪʃər] mass of ice moving slowly down a mountain valley – 32 **to exert** to bring into use, to exercise – **tug** sudden hard pull

67   10 **exertion** energetic activity, effort – 31 **clumsy** without skill, not making movements properly – 39 **droopy** which hang down – 40 **coated** covered

68   2 **grit** tiny, hard bits of sand, stone, etc. – 13 **ledger** *here:* book listing reservations – 21 **to linger** to stay – 27 **napkin** piece of cloth used at meals for protecting clothes or wiping the lips – 33 **tempting** attractive – 39 **to hover** to remain in the air at one place

69 1 **lobster** shellfish with eight legs which is red when boiled – 7 **vocation** true profession to which one feels called – 8 **to broil** to grill – 11 **film** thin coating or covering – **gauzy** ['gɔːzɪ] thin, almost transparent – **panel** piece of material of some kind – 14 **veil** [eɪ] covering of fine net, usually used to hide a woman's face – **to yank** to pull violently

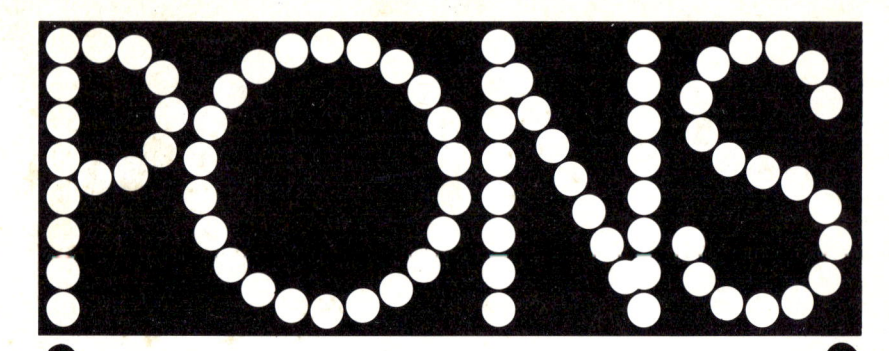

PONS-Reisewörterbuch Englisch
(Klettbuch 51861)
Sprachführer und Wörterbuch zugleich,
über 200 Seiten und 5000 Stichwörter.

PONS-Taschenwörterbuch Englisch
(Klettbuch 51711)
Klein, praktisch, über 700 Seiten,
rund 35 000 Stichwörter, paßt in jede Tasche.

PONS-Kompaktwörterbuch Englisch
(Klettbuch 5171)
75 000 Stichwörter, 40 000 Wendungen,
kompakt im Format, universell einsetzbar, unerläßliches
Wörterbuch zum Lernen und Nachschlagen.

PONS-Globalwörterbuch Englisch
(Klettbuch 51713, 51714)
Besonders umfassend im Wortschatz, getrennt in zwei
Bänden mit jeweils 80 000 Stichwörtern pro Sprach-
richtung.

PONS-Großwörterbuch Englisch
(Klettbuch 51715)
Neu entwickeltes Wörterbuch von Collins mit 220 000
Stichwörtern.

PONS-Wörterbücher von Klett sind in jeder guten
Buchhandlung erhältlich.

Punkt für Punkt zuverlässig.